Breaking the Chains of Abuse

For David

ACKNOWLEDGMENTS

Many people helped in the writing of this book. It was within the Greenbelt Arts Festival Survivors' Group that I gained the confidence to consider starting it. Thank you Concetta for introducing me to that group and for teaching me about assertiveness and forgiveness. Thank you Kirsty for leading brilliant sessions, Charlotte for friendship and for showing me I could be a princess too, Jane for so many things, especially for support during the editing process. Thank you Melanie and Abi for help with the chapter on dissociating and thanks to the Bristol Crisis Service for Women for help with dealing with flashbacks.

It has been a privilege to get to know the amazingly strong people I've met through S:VOX and Mayumarri in Australia. You've inspired me and taught me so much about breaking the chains of abuse. Thanks especially to Wendy who taught me how to scream and to Liz for showing me that I could heal.

Thank you John and Ruth for guiding me through those tortuous early stages. I will for ever be grateful for your considerable professional skills.

I couldn't have managed to complete this book without the support of my 'sisterhood' friends – Jane again, Sue, Elaine, Julie, Julie, Alice, Anne, Meriel and of course Kate, whose drawings of my creatures captured their characters and whose steadfast friendship and wisdom added so much to my own thinking and therefore to this book.

Thank you to my family, Jonathan, Rachel, Nick and Liz who are generous with their support and love – and of course David, who is always there.

Thank you all.

Sue Atkinson

Breaking the Chains of Abuse

A PRACTICAL GUIDE

Sue Atkinson

LION

A Lion Book
an imprint of
Lion Hudson plc
Mayfield House, 256 Banbury Road,
Oxford OX2 7DH, England
www.lionhudson.com
ISBN 978 0 7459 5135 5
ISBN 0 7459 5135 X

First edition 2006
10 9 8 7 6 5 4 3 2 1 0

The text paper used in this book has been made from wood
independently certified as having come from sustainable forests.

A catalogue record for this book is available
from the British Library

Typeset in 10.5/12pt Berkeley Old Style Book
Printed and bound in Great Britain
by Cox & Wyman Ltd, Reading

Contents

Introduction

This book is for:

- people who have experienced abuse, particularly sexual abuse

- both male and female, adult and child victims/survivors

- parents and other supporters of abuse victims who want to know more about the effects of abuse in order to care more effectively

- people in leadership positions, such as teachers, health and social workers and clergy, who need information about abuse.

This book is especially for people like these friends of mine who are survivors of abuse:

- Flick, who is struggling because she has to stop therapy and she doesn't know how she will cope.

- Helen, who had a T-shirt made with 'Silent no more' on the front and 'I was sexually abused' on the back.

- Richard, who has lost two stone and has another eight to lose. He started to comfort eat after he was raped ten years ago.

- Laura, who was told that if she put on weight she would be given help. So she put on weight only to find that the 'help' was a totally unsuitable mixed gender and mixed needs group 'therapy', where she could not talk about her abuse. She has been told that if she stops going to the group (it is destroying all her confidence) she will get no more help at all.

- Lucy, who is trying desperately hard to stop self-harming.

- Ali, who became so ill after he was attacked that he became depressed and had to give up his job. He's been unemployed for six years and is finding it hard to convince employers to take him on.

- Claire, who says: 'I often think of a little gremlin sat on my shoulder whispering negative things in my ear. He tells me I'm a waste of space and a bad person who isn't worth bothering about. He's very good at popping up when I'm at my lowest!'

A communication problem

The trouble with abuse is that abused people don't much like talking or writing about what happened to them, and those who haven't been abused find the whole thing so upsetting that they don't want to hear or read about it.

I hope I can solve at least some of this problem of communication by writing honestly and openly about what happened to me and to other survivors. (I've used the term 'survivor' as shorthand for people who were abused. I know some people don't like it much, for all kinds of good reasons, but it is such common shorthand that most people will know what I mean. It signifies the move we make, with help, from being a victim to being someone who is trying to heal. And it feels true to my daily life; I just about survive – with help.)

The statistics

The statistics for child abuse, adult rape and sexual assault and adult domestic violence are shocking. Some recent research from the UK and the USA gives the following figures:

• One in four girls and one in nine boys experience some kind of abuse in childhood.

• One in eight women and one in twelve men report that they were sexually abused before the age of sixteen.

• One female in four experiences domestic violence at some point in her life.

• One male in nine is abused at some time in his life. (But we know that the figures for men represent considerable under-reporting by men and some say it is at least one man in seven and probably more than that).

• In the UK in 1999 over one in three female murder victims were killed by their present or former partner.

• The NSPCC says that in the UK, more than one child dies each week as a result of abuse by an adult.

• In the USA it is estimated that there are 60 million survivors. That's about 20 per cent of the population, or one in five people.

• Statistics vary, but it seems that a huge percentage of the prison population were abused as children.

As I've trawled through books and research reports to verify statistics, one phrase crops up again and again:

'Our results show only the tip of the iceberg because most abuse is not reported.'

Although I know that more people are abused than is generally recognized, I feel deeply shaken by these statistics.

It's time for the abusers to be afraid, because the culture of secrecy and silence that they need is being smashed apart as researchers shout to the world that all is not well.

Ways to use this book

• This book contains practical ideas to help you to recover from the traumatic effects of abuse.

• It is a book to 'do' as much as to read, so you might want to read it all the way through or you might prefer just to dip into activities that suit your needs at that moment. (For example, finding coping strategies for dealing with panic and so on.)

• You will get more from it if you treat it as a 'workbook' and actually do some of the activities, so you will need a range of pens and pencils, and at least one notebook.

• You can develop some of the activities with crayons and paints etc. But if that doesn't grab you, just miss those bits out and come back to them later.

• If you have a supporter you could tell them you are reading the book. Sharing some of your work with them might help you to make considerable progress.

• Focusing on the trauma can start to give us some power to change our own lives. We can't sit around and wait for other people to change our lives. That doesn't work.

• We are the ones who must change our lives, in our own way and in our own time. It is a long slow process, but the activities in this book are designed to help you to get back the power in your life that you lost because of abuse.

Your own plan for using this book and keeping safe

• You might want to plan to have a safe place where you can read without interruptions. Keeping ourselves safe is crucial.

• The book is likely to raise issues that are uncomfortable, so you might want to plan to get more support, perhaps by joining a self-help group (see the resources section at the back). This is particularly important if you don't feel you have enough support now.

• Go slowly, respecting your own needs, and doing only what you can manage in one sitting. Find appropriate coping strategies within the book that you most need at that moment. (These are listed in the contents.)

You've had the courage and strength to survive this far – so you can do it. You can break those chains that hold you in fear and pain.

A 'health warning'

I've tried to write an accessible book that tells the truth about the awfulness of abuse, but I found that to do that I couldn't make it a 'trigger-free' book – I couldn't eliminate everything from it that might be upsetting to some people. What 'triggers' painful feelings for one person might be OK for another.

So look above at the plans for keeping yourself safe. If you feel yourself being triggered, stop and go for some self-pampering when the going gets tough: ask for a hug, eat some chocolate, or go for a calming walk – whatever will comfort you.

The structure of the book

I found that my cuddly creatures helped me to acknowledge bits of myself that are hurt or angry or afraid, and they became very important to me in my healing. I've used some of them to show the stages I went through, starting with Pooh Bear and Old Eeyore.

Pooh Bear and Old Eeyore

Part 1

The start of it all

• •

This section introduces the effects that abuse of any kind can cause. It outlines the new understandings we have of trauma, gives some details of the common symptoms of abuse and outlines some of the problems that can arise such as memory confusions and depression.

*I've always hated it in movies and plays, the woman who is ripped open by
violence and then asked to parcel out redemption for the rest of her life.
'I forgive you,' I said. I said what I had to. I would die by pieces
to save myself from real death.
He perked up. Looked at me. 'You're a beautiful girl,' he said.*

ALICE SEBOLD

1 Wallowing in it?

I was just finishing off leading a seminar about creative writing at a Christian arts festival and was chatting to someone whom I had known for many years.

'Must go now,' I said to her. 'Time for survivors' group.' She looked at me with a pained look on her face.

'Ugh,' she said, 'how can you have those meetings without people wallowing in that kind of thing?'

My initial reaction was to be stunned. Do some people really still think like that?

A source of strength

The survivors' meetings at this arts festival had become important to me. They were where I found a group of people who understood what I was going through – where I was learning how to handle my life despite emotions that seemed at times to be out of control. The people in that group had become such a support to me that I eventually found the strength to write this book.

'Wallowing in it'?

I don't think so – at least I hope not!

So I told my friend about abuse and what it feels like, even years later. By the time I had finished talking to her, she had a look of total amazement on her face. She was the one who was now stunned. Many people just do not know what the results of abuse can sometimes be.

The need to avoid 'wallowing in it' (inappropriately focusing on the fact that we are chained up rather than trying to break chains) has become an important thread in my thinking as I write this book.

'It's all in the past – move on.'

Yes, the abuse (for some people) is in the past, and yes, 'people need to move on'. 'It's the future that matters.'

Yes, I agree with all that – of course. At one level no one could dispute it.

BUT…

- I'm quite sure that some people have no idea about the power and impact abuse has on someone's life.

- Abusers want us all to keep it quiet. It is in their interest for people to refuse to engage with the problems survivors face. Silence and secrecy are important aspects of abusers' methods. So I want to speak out about abuse – without wallowing.

For many of us, 'moving on' is a terrible struggle. We are chained up in the confusions and complexities of emotions we do not understand and that seem so excruciatingly difficult to break away from.

We want to be healed.

We want to be free from the past and able to walk in the sunshine without the guilt.

But it is so very hard.

Activities to help break our chains

I've tried to analyse the kinds of problems that survivors face, but I also set out to focus on practical solutions to our problems and I have included these at the end of each chapter.

Some of these practical solutions you might not like – such as writing in a journal – but I hope that you will do some of the activities, because we learn and we change by doing things. This is how we can change our thinking and behaviour and break our chains.

But there is a right time to do those activities. If you don't fancy doing them today, go back to them later. Make this book a workbook – something you interact with and not just words on a page that you read.

If you can try out some of these things, I truly believe that you will be breaking some of the chains that trap you in confusion and unhappiness, and that you will begin to feel at least some sense of empowerment. (By this I mean a sense of having at least some control over our lives when we can make informed choices and escape the grip and legacy of our abusers.)

Most of all I hope this book will lead to that empowerment – to your chains being broken.

Writing, drawing, painting, hugging, and talking to my creatures did that for me.

KEY POINTS

■ Many people don't understand the devastating effects of any kind of abuse.

■ Moving on can be difficult, but we can break the chains of abuse that keep us trapped in unhappiness and confusion.

CHAIN BREAKING

1. Look back at the section 'Ways to use this book' on page 9. Think about your own plan for working through this book.

You *must* find a safe place. Feeling safe is so crucial to chain breaking. I curl up beside or in my bed and wrap myself in a fleecy blanket and cuddle Eeyore.

2. In your safe place create a list of what to do if you feel overwhelmed or suicidal. This is likely to include phone numbers, or things to do, or places to go. Make a few copies of your list and put them where you will see them.

3. You might want to gather around you a few more supporters. It's good if you have at least one person or organization that you can ring in an emergency. In the UK we have the Samaritans (see the resources section at the end of the book). Remember that not all our friends want phone calls in the middle of the night! But if we know there is someone we can phone or text, it can soothe the worst moments. (If you are saying to yourself that you don't know any more possible supporters, then join a self-help group, such as S:VOX in the UK. There is a list in the resources section.)

4. Get a journal or a pad of paper to draw, scribble or write on and a folder to keep your work in. (Keep your work in a safe place.)

Many therapists now use writing as a path to healing, but if that freaks you out try other alternatives such as drawing, painting or using children's modelling materials. There are suggestions of things to do as you go through the book and it is really important that you note your progress in some way. Otherwise you might not notice the progress you are making in breaking your chains.

Knowing *and remembering* that we're making progress is crucial.

You're reading this book so that's a good place to start. You could write, 'I'm on the way to breaking my chains' on a sticky note and put it where you will see it every day.

5. You could seek out your old teddy or get yourself a cuddly creature from a charity shop.

Remember
Take care of yourself – go gently through the book. If it becomes too much, just stop for a while and do something you enjoy. Little and often might be a good plan.

Feel the fear and do it anyway.
SUSAN JEFFERS

2 All abuse hurts

Any form of abuse can leave victims emotionally confused, sometimes for many years, and although it can seem that sexual abuse is the worst kind, people who work with survivors claim that sometimes abuse that isn't sexual can do as much, if not *more*, long-term damage than sexual abuse.

So this book is about all kinds of abuse, partly because that reflects the experience of many people. Sometimes abuse can be:

- physical
- emotional/psychological
- spiritual
- sexual

It includes:

- bullying
- domestic violence
- neglect and abandonment – both of which can be traumatic to a child.

It's probably obvious that physical abuse involves acts such as hitting, biting, burning, kicking and so on, but emotional and sexual abuse are harder to define. We need to clarify what is included in these forms of abuse before we continue.

Emotional abuse

A few years ago I wouldn't have recognized that much of my abuse as a child was emotional/psychological. But all the 'putting down' by my birth family, my abandonment, and my mother's 'emotional blackmail' were all significant factors in my growing up to believe I was 'hopeless'.

It seems to me that some kind of emotional cruelty is present during *any* abuse – and *any* abuse is an abuse of power. So a domineering, bullying or manipulative boss, doctor, minister or parent and so on can be abusing their power in any situation, causing a sense of powerlessness in the victim and setting up a chain reaction of emotional problems, from low self-esteem to suicide.

Sexual abuse
In both adults and children some aspects of sexual abuse are obvious, but there is much that wouldn't be obvious to the non-abusing world.

I had absolutely no idea that an adult could sexually abuse a baby or a toddler, or that there were many ways in which they might do that. Presumably this is part of the content of those illegal websites that some paedophiles organize and visit.

Child sexual abuse includes fondling the child, or making a child touch the adult's genitals, and/or involving the child in masturbation.

As well as penetration of the child (including the anus and mouth) with an object, a finger or the penis, there are also non-contact aspects, such as exposing genitals, making a child watch sex or look at pornographic pictures, or involving the child in pornography.

> *[Sexual abuse involves] encouraging children to behave in sexually inappropriate ways,[and emotional abuse] may involve causing children frequently to feel frightened or in danger, or the exploitation or corruption of children.*
> JANE CHEVOUS

Mild abuse?
In general I don't think there is such a thing as 'mild abuse'. But I suppose teasing could be thought of as 'mild abuse' when it gets out of hand, or the recipient just cannot cope with it. ('What's wrong? Can't you take a joke?')

• Bullying at school can have a huge impact on a child.

• Bullying in the workplace can throw competent professionals into a world of chaos.

• A naked 'flasher' in the park can have an enormous effect on a child, or on adults who have 'hidden memories' (they have 'forgotten' them) of other unpleasant sexual instances. And that 'enormous effect' is likely to be misunderstood and to lead to the 'pull yourself together' comments that do even more damage.

It seems that the golden rule when thinking about the severity of abuse is not to assess what *you* think the impact on someone might be ('Oh, that was nothing, move on,'), but to realize that the impact of an abusive act relates to the meaning it had to the victim *at the time*, and then try to understand the ways in which that victim has tried to cope.

So for me, despite the awful things that my step-father did to me, I'm far more confused and angry with my uncle, who 'just' held my breasts and laughed at me when I was a teenager on holiday with him in Scotland.

Holding my breasts probably seems minor, but to an already confused fourteen-year-old, that repeated act by my only adult male blood relative (who I'm sure knew about my step-father's cruelty, particularly to my mother) had a devastating effect. I adored this uncle and still cannot sort out the confusion that I feel. (Last week when someone asked me when I was first depressed I said, 'About fourteen or fifteen.' I made a connection. Did I first become depressed following that summer holiday with my uncle?)

So an important principle for supporting survivors is not to label some abuse as 'mild', but to seek to find out what the impact was on the survivors at the time by listening to them now.

My story
Throughout the book runs a story that has mainly taken place over the eighteen years since my memories of childhood sexual abuse (and the associated physical and emotional abuse) returned.

I was having therapy with John because of a traumatic and abusive work situation that I was in involving a head teacher. I was her deputy head and, as she said to one of my colleagues, she was going to 'make life so difficult for Sue that she'll want to leave'. So she set in motion a most appalling abuse of power.

I fell apart and became suicidal.

I sat with John trying to put my life back together again and to sort out why such intense bullying had left me in a crumpled heap – at one point unable even to walk, which was terrifying, followed by a few days when I couldn't see properly.

I knew that something had struck at the core of my being.

I developed many really difficult phobias and spent years refusing to accept that these images were 'hidden memories' of childhood sexual abuse – though the evidence that they were was mounting up.

I thought I knew why I had some sexual problems and a fear of men. I was 'raped' by a stranger in the park when I was six. I remember every moment of that, and the aftermath when my mother did some of her disastrous mothering. She rang the police, but she told me to stay in the other room and she kept coming in to question me, then going back to the phone to tell them a bit more, then coming back to me and so on.

'Did the man put his willie inside your knickers?' 'Yes.' I had intense feelings of shame, especially when I showed her the six pennies the man had given me. The look of horror on her face told me I had done something very bad. She took the pennies from me; my longing for a six-penny bar of chocolate disappeared.

At no time did my mother hug or comfort me. I was left to wash myself and to retreat to my room, ashamed – and without the comfort of my chocolate.

So as an adult, I told myself there was nothing in the weird images and phobias that appeared from nowhere. To think that there was just proved what an evil person I was.

Finding Ruth
When we moved to London, after some confusing sessions with a couple of psychiatrists and an energetic young GP who wanted me to go and see yet another psychiatrist, I eventually found Ruth with whom I worked for six years. She described herself as a 'psychodynamic therapist' and I liked her very much from the start.

For most of my time with Ruth I refused to believe that 'anything happened', and much of this book shows my struggle to accept that I was abused and my attempts to break the chains of the phobias that ruled my life.

I felt as if I was chained up, and however much I tried to break the chains they just got tighter around my legs so I couldn't walk. All I could do was struggle – but the chains grew round my arms and my body and I just wanted to lie down and die.

Breaking the chains with creatures
When I started therapy with Ruth it was natural to take along Eeyore, my favourite cuddly creature, and introduce him to Ruth, explaining his significance to me. Amazingly Ruth is a cuddlies person too and as we worked together we found that the creatures were crucial in the healing process.

When at last I found the courage to go to a survivors' group in London, I saw that lots of survivors had cuddlies just as I did.

Our teddies and other creatures can reflect something of our personality and that is why some of us need lots of them. I loved Eeyore for his view on life – always expecting life to be a bit unfair, but

making the best of it anyway with a good sense of humour. He is able to retreat gloomily to his own little patch and leave his friends to their socializing and frolics. He knows life is tough, but puts up with calamities – like losing his tail and even his house – with good grace.

I found it comforting to hang on to Eeyore at night when I was afraid, or during panic attacks, or bouts of weeping. Somehow Eeyore could bring a moment of relief, a sense that life would go on, and that I could somehow try to climb up out of the darkness of depression.

My mother threw away my toys when I was about eight, including Rabbit, my friend and ally against the world.

But for my twenty-first birthday, some friends gave me a real teddy, with jointed arms and legs. He is Pooh Bear, who has very little brain but hums his way through life. Not ever having had a teddy, this gift was one that helped me to start facing the truth. I'd had a pretty awful childhood and I was determined to get beyond that.

When I had to leave therapy with Ruth (because David, my partner, changed jobs and we moved to Norwich), I became friends with Kate. She became one of my supporters and it was natural to ask her to draw the creatures as we explored a way forward for this book.

Searching for healing

I've linked my story with the stories that other survivors have allowed me to share. I've sat in survivor self-help groups, seminars, healing sessions and lectures about abuse. I've read widely about the experiences of a great many survivors and through these varied experiences – and therapy with John and Ruth – I've come up with some factors that seem to be general for most survivors, such as our crucial need to have a safe place we can escape to.

I've sought out healing situations in a variety of ways – classes in developing self-esteem and assertiveness, for example – and I've even travelled to Australia to be part of a healing week recommended by two survivors I know. (That week was a real 'wow', with chains being smashed apart all over the place.)

Coping strategies

Throughout the book there are lists of 'coping strategies', and you can add any of these to your 'safe place list' (suggested at the end of chapter one) as you work through the book.

Coping strategies get us through the next ten minutes, then the next. If you self-harm as a way of coping, don't worry too much about that at the moment. As you get stronger and work through this book, gradually you will find the strength to move on.

One really important coping strategy is not to 'beat ourselves up' about the things that we do to survive.

Another major coping strategy, as mentioned in the previous chapter, is to have a safe place where you can just 'be'. If you haven't found that safe place yet, make that a priority.

KEY POINTS

- All abuse hurts.

- Apparently 'mild' abuse can be devastating.

- Cuddly creatures can help us to heal.

- Find a safe place where you can just 'be'.

CHAIN BREAKING

1. Write, paint or draw your reactions to reading this chapter. For example, you could list the kinds of abuse you were subjected to. If you only have vague memories or 'images', use them to write/draw/paint.

2. As you do these activities you do need to keep yourself safe. It's normal to be angry and to cry in response to thinking about what people did to you.

3. Did you work at getting more supporters? It will be tough going to work through this book totally on your own.

4. Did you seek out your old teddy, or find a creature in a charity shop?

Remember
By working through this book you are going to take back control over your life and over the feelings that you lost through the abuse.

> *The healing is a life long process – but – the light does shine in the darkness and what is more the darkness has never put it out.*
> MARGARET KENNEDY

3 Problems with trauma

The symptoms experienced by people who have been abused are many and varied. Some might just have one or two on the following list, but most people I've talked to have several. (This isn't a complete list.) These symptoms can include:

• 'flashbacks' – sudden memories crashing into our head at unexpected times

• disturbing thoughts, sometimes these are 'racing thoughts'

• compulsions including self-harming and eating problems, and sometimes this gets so bad it becomes Obsessive Compulsive Disorder – obsessions and fears that have become so extreme that they lock you into a pattern of behaviour that can seriously chain you down and rule your life

• nightmares or other sleep disturbances such as waking up screaming

• excessive fear, for example a fear of going to sleep or going out of the house; many survivors have a fear of having people behind them

• hallucinations, including 'seeing' or 'hearing' the abuser when he/she isn't present

• being in a state of hyper-vigilance (on 'red alert') – this can tend to make people jumpy and irritable, which has a knock-on effect on those around us

• difficulties with relationships, particularly with sexual relationships, such as a fear of sex and sometimes confusion over sexual orientation

• extreme panic and anxiety in a wide range of contexts including social contexts, for example, facing crowds in cinemas, restaurants or churches

• experiencing wild mood swings

• emotional difficulties such as being unable to trust people, or the reverse of that – over-trusting people who are not trustworthy

• low self-esteem, lack of confidence, putting ourselves down, always apologizing, which sometimes leads to paranoia

- hostility, anger and difficulties with authority, sometimes leading to criminal behaviour

- feelings of guilt, such as 'I'm a really bad person – the world would be a better place if I didn't exist'

- a tendency to move from one abusive relationship to another

- frequent bouts of depression

- feeling powerless and unable to change the situation.

As you work through the book it is this last point that will be challenged the most. The suggested activities will help you to acknowledge these awful symptoms and plan how to break free of them. It is possible to change.

Learning about trauma

I began to find out more about trauma through reading some books by Herman, Rothschild and Cozolino (see the resources section). I recommend all three books to those who want more of a theoretical understanding of how abuse affects people.

Judith Herman's well-researched book changed my thinking. In the back of my mind was the fear of 'wallowing in it'. I was struggling to break free from the phobias that meant I couldn't live a 'normal' life. Everything I did had to be planned like some military battle with escape routes thought through in advance, every eventuality covered, and some tranquillizers ready.

I saw myself as hopeless and pathetic. 'I'm safe with David,' I'd say to myself. 'It's all in the past – get over it.'

But the fears and phobias haunted me. They ruled my life.

Post-Traumatic Stress Disorder

I came to understand that all the different labels I'd been given by the medical profession (manic depression and so on) were maybe only part of the truth. What had not been diagnosed was that I was suffering from Post-Traumatic Stress Disorder (PTSD).

Reading Judith Herman's book was a Damascus Road experience for me – the light of truth shone onto my chains.

My symptoms from childhood through to adulthood were those of PTSD.

My difficulties in breaking the chains of abuse were not difficulties that arose because I was pathetic, but because trauma just is difficult to escape from!

It's all in your head

Apparently memories of traumatic incidents are stored in our brain in a different way from happier memories, and in childhood trauma the development of the brain is badly affected.

> *Childhood trauma compromises neural networks.*
> LOUIS COZOLINO

What these researchers seem to be saying is that our bad memories get locked into our brain in such a way that they are very difficult to unlock; there aren't the brain pathways needed for that.

> *[Traumatic memories] are stored in more primitive circuits... [so]... they*
> *are strongly somatic, sensory, and emotional, as well as inherently nonverbal.*
> *[This] results in an absence of the memory in time, so when it is triggered it*
> *is experienced as occurring in the present.*
> LOUIS COZOLINO

Not wallowing but drowning

So as I write this book I'm trying to show that as survivors we try to move on. We try to live for the future and not dwell on the past.

But the nature of trauma is that it is hard to recover from – we need to learn and be helped to unlock those trapped memories. And of course that is a long and difficult process.

Abuse can cause trauma. It's not like falling off your bike and grazing your knee. It can be a lifelong struggle to unlock the trauma and get beyond the flashbacks, the nightmares and that lurking guilt and shame we feel. It's more like trying to avoid drowning.

Speaking the unspeakable

In the introduction to her book, Judith Herman points out that:

> *The ordinary response to atrocities is to banish them from consciousness.*
> *Certain violations... are too terrible to utter aloud: this is the meaning of the*
> *word **unspeakable**. (Judith's emphasis.)*

The use of the word 'atrocities' interested me in this book about trauma. I thought this was far too strong a word at first. But as I read on, I realized that I would be happy for that word to be used of some of the things that have happened to other survivors, although I felt I couldn't use it of my own experiences.

However, I began to see that I was denying the strength of my own feelings, denying that it hurt that much, denying how bad I felt inside.

I keep doing that.

I recognize it in other survivors.

'It's unspeakable, so let's keep it all low key, nothing I can't handle.' But I still feel bad inside. I still feel unable to face life.

So I tell myself I am pathetic.

We don't want to speak it – it's so much easier and more comfortable to tell ourselves that we are feeble and useless – so we try to bury it inside. But as Judith Herman says, 'Atrocities refuse to be buried.'

The outcomes of trauma

In some ways it was reassuring to find that abuse can be seen as being as traumatic as other events, such as being a soldier at war, or being tortured or imprisoned. But it was also scary.

It's not difficult to understand why a little seven-year-old boy I used to teach was traumatized. He had arrived in England from Africa to be with relatives after seeing his parents and siblings hacked to death in front of him.

Everything we hear about the trenches in the First World War shows us that soldiers were being quite 'normal' to tremble and be 'shell shocked'. And how did people cope with losing a child, a parent, a fiancé or a partner?

That is also unspeakable. I cannot write a sentence that would adequately say what I would feel if one of my children, or David, died.

How can we deal with such trauma?

We may do something like this:

• At a funeral service, if anyone shows even the slightest sign of being upset, someone will hiss loudly at them, 'Chin up. Mustn't let the side down.'

• Behave like they do in soap operas, so when someone has just faced a deeply traumatic event such as a miscarriage, or their partner has just died in a house fire, another character will say to them, 'Well, it all happened in the past and now we have to move on.' (This means 'Don't ever mention the trauma again'.)

But what those who write about trauma are saying is that whether it is terror experienced during war, or bomb blasts, or ethnic cleansing, or imprisonment, or torture – whatever the devastating event – the response is trauma, and the recovery is usually slow and difficult.

Abuse is put alongside all of these life-changing events. Yes, presumably some people cope with abuse well. But some don't. Especially when the abuse is prolonged and repeated.

The outcomes of these traumas have common threads and the recovery process also has many common features. So as I said in chapter two, whatever kind of abuse it was, you are likely to have the same symptoms as people who were abused in different ways from you, and the recovery strategies can be similar.

Of course there will be some aspects of your abuse and how you are now that are specific to what happened to you. Male rape, for example, is devastating, and is compounded by some men feeling unable to report what happened, and maybe even feeling a bit 'sissy' if they cry. These survivors may struggle to hold down their job or go to the pub with their mates. They may feel held down by the chains of what our society expects of men.

The stages of recovery
Whatever the abuse, it looks as if there are common features of recovery for everyone. I really like the three-fold process of unpacking hurts that some psychologists describe as:

1. Uncovery

2. Discovery

3. Recovery

First we have to uncover what has happened. Blurred mental images and strange body feelings have almost no meaning at first; we have to do some 'uncovery'.

As we uncover, so we discover. We eventually work out what that recurring dream is about. We come to understand why we react so strongly to people kissing on television – or any number of the things that freak us out. These first two stages can go on for ages and may only gradually blend into some sense of recovery.

This three-fold process is very close to the discovery stages suggested by Judith Herman, which she identifies as:

- Establishing safety. (Yes! We must feel safe or we will not feel able to 'uncover'.)

- Reconstructing the traumatic events so that they make some kind of sense. (This is 'uncovery' and 'discovery'.)

- Restoring the connections between survivors and their community. (A good definition of 'recovery'.)

Abuse doesn't just affect the victim

Abuse always has an effect on the survivor's community – that is, their family, their friends and anyone who plays a part in the survivor's life.

There is some evidence that, for a supporter of a survivor, hearing any detail of the abuse can be as traumatic as the abuse itself. So the parents of a child or adult rape victim struggle with life along with the survivor.

The whole community is likely to be in shock when abuse is disclosed, and it only helps the perpetrators if we keep silent. Abuse thrives in secrecy and pretence, so rather than disguising what has happened it is better for the family or other community to talk about it openly.

> [Abuse] symptoms could be alleviated when the traumatic memories, as well as the intense feelings that accompanied them, were recovered and put into words. This method of treatment became the basis of modern psychotherapy… the 'talking cure'.
>
> JUDITH HERMAN

Words and feelings

Words are important, very important. Whether you write them, speak them or think them – as you paint, draw or dig the garden – it is words that will unravel those chains, *as well as touching the feelings* that we had at the time of the abuse.

This is the kind of process that researchers such as Louis Cozolino seem to be saying can get our brain connections to unlock those trapped memories. He calls it 'neural network integration'.

For some, the words come more easily than the feelings. That's OK. Let the words flow – or if they won't flow, jump on cans to crush the feelings or dance to loud music.

In places in this book I've used some 'Inner Child' work because this helps us to touch and unlock the childhood (or adult) emotions that we felt at the time of the abuse, but which we have 'buried' because those emotions were unspeakable and unthinkable. Breaking chains means feeling those hurts, acknowledging how bad they felt, and then empowering that little hurt child within us (who is there even if we were abused as an adult) so that we can move on and recover.

But all that means we must *do* things. Just reading this book is OK for now, but if you feel strong enough, have a go at chain breaking.

Strategies for dealing with panic and anxiety

1. Panic and anxiety feelings are there because too much adrenalin is pumping around your body. Try to breathe deeply and slowly, counting to five as you breathe in and counting to five as you breathe out. Imagine all the bad feelings being pushed out of your body as you breathe out. (Be careful that in your panic you don't breathe too quickly in the mistaken belief that you are not getting enough air into your lungs. If we breathe in too much air we end up light headed and tingly. Slow down your breathing.)

2. Exercise seems to reduce the impact of adrenalin, so put on loud music and dance it out of your system. (If you have dental treatment, ask for the pain-killing injections without adrenalin.)

3. To get rid of the sense of tension, do some relaxation exercises (lie down if you can but you can do them standing up). Tense up every muscle in your body one at a time. Tense your feet, then release; tense your legs, then release; and so on.

4. Be aware of when the bad feelings start. What triggered them just at that moment? Identifying triggers can help us to feel we're making progress.

5. Feeling anxious all day can be tackled by taking time out to relax, but it would be a good idea to see your doctor.

6. Panic attacks are different from that all-day anxiety. An attack is distinctive: an inability to breathe normally; a pounding heart; an intense feeling that we might not survive this; and sometimes dizziness and nausea. It's important to tell your doctor.

7. The most crucial thing to do is to accept that this is a panic attack and you are not going to die. Breathe deeply, say your mantra ('I'm OK, this is a panic attack, I'm not going to die'), and ask yourself what triggered it if you can. If not, leave that until you are stronger.

8. Bad days are normal. Focus on your good days and believe the good days will become more numerous as you get better at handling your panic.

9. Suffering from overwhelming fear is normal – it's not an illness and you *can* get rid of the panic and anxiety. Share it at your self-help group. The book by Dr Roger Baker in the resources section is helpful.

KEY POINTS

■ Symptoms of abuse that we are left with are varied and can be hugely powerful in our lives, so we can feel chained up and powerless.

■ Abuse can cause trauma and, just as soldiers at war can suffer from PTSD, so can abuse victims. We are struggling to recover, not wallowing.

■ Writing, drawing and other activities can help us to work through our feelings – a necessary process if we are to recover.

CHAIN BREAKING

1. Have you got your safe place? It really will help.

2. Look back to the three stages outlined on pages 29 and 30 and think which stage or stages you might be at. (You are likely to be at more than one.)

3. Try to write, draw or paint some of the feelings you have now – maybe your reactions to reading this chapter. For example, you might be surprised that PTSD could be what you are struggling with, rather than being lazy or pathetic, or whatever you or those around you say.

4. If you recognize some of your symptoms from the list at the start of this chapter, you might want to note down the ones that give you the most trouble. You could focus on those and learn some strategies for dealing with them as you work through the book.

5. You do need to tell your story in a variety of ways. You might want to tell your story in words or pictures or both. Huge bits of paper and thick brushes or pens can be a great help.

6. Look at the quote below. At some point you are going to need to talk and share your feelings and your story.

Remember
Recovery from trauma is demanding, so take time out. Do something soothing such as going swimming, walking in the park, listening to music, drinking herbal tea or reading a children's story book.

> *The core experiences of psychological trauma are disempowerment and disconnection from others. Recovery, therefore, is based upon the empowerment of the survivor and the creation of new connections. Recovery can take place only within the context of relationships; it cannot occur in isolation.*
> JUDITH HERMAN

4 Problems with memory

Because so many of my memories of early childhood abuse had become deeply buried inside me and mostly forgotten, I had considerable problems with seeing these strange 'images' and 'part memories' that were crashing into my head as being anything significant – let alone memories of abuse. I was convinced that I was 'making it all up', so proving that I was evil and that the world would be a better place if I were dead – an idea that had haunted me for many years and that was the basis of my suicide attempts.

Was I making it up?

Distrusting these terrifying images, my mind was plunged into chaos. Were these images all a fantasy? Had someone somehow planted the idea in my head? Had I planted the whole idea in my own head? (Apparently it is very rare for people to make up abuse.)

My painful journey through these thoughts (a journey that still goes on) runs throughout this book and I focus on it because so many survivors struggle with these difficult issues – indeed if you look on the web you might think that 'false memory syndrome' is the *only* issue about abuse. (Those who support the idea of 'false memory syndrome' want to say that most people who claim to have been abused have got it wrong. This is what our abusers very much hope we will all believe.)

For years I declared that I was 'making it all up'. I knew I needed support because my life was falling apart. The only way I could survive was to keep busy – so busy that I frequently had to stop completely because of burnout and depression. The trouble was that if I stopped and lay in bed crying, I had too much time to think about what was in my head, so I needed to get better quickly and get back out there and back to work.

I developed dangerously high blood pressure. I cried most days. I suffered from terrible 'racing thoughts' – thoughts that go through my head so fast that it is very scary and feels as if they will never stop and I will go mad. ('You made it all up, you are evil, but what about that flashback yesterday? It must have been about something.') Had it not been for my loving family and my little dog, Jemma, I'm not sure I would have made it through this 'emergency stage'.

But I'm jumping ahead in the story. That 'emergency stage' was at its very worst when I was working with Ruth. It was during these times that I began to realise with horror that I might have to take the scary images seriously.

It gets worse

It's important to note that for most survivors I know, things get worse and worse at first before there is any improvement. Usually there is some trigger for this – mine included the bullying head teacher, which somehow set off something inside me about abuse of power. So early childhood memories of being abused emerged – and I had had no conscious memory of these at all. So when people say to us, 'You were fine two years ago, why are you like this now?', it is hard to give an answer because we wonder why too.

Why is what happened to us so long ago suddenly getting in the way of normal life?

Why are we getting worse and not better?

Buried memories

I think the key to why things get worse is that our buried memories are so deep within us that of course it is painful to deal with them. We buried them because they were too painful to deal with at the time they happened.

I have a friend who remains completely convinced that these memories are best left buried. I wish she were right! But I don't think she is. The times when my memories were buried were some of the most painful of the whole of my life – times of deep depression, suicidal thinking, and devastating fear that led to being in a state of panic all day.

It was awful.

But it's been awful letting the memories come to the surface too, so I completely understand when some survivors make it clear that they don't want to go on with understanding what is behind their chaotic life. They just want to bury it all again and get back to keeping it all hidden. I tried this. It took a huge amount of effort to keep things buried and I'm sure that this was the cause of my panic and depression metamorphosing into compulsions, phobias, nightmares and flashbacks that were out of control.

(If you want just to bury it all again, perhaps because you are in crisis, that is what you need to do for now. Seek out something comforting for yourself and skip forward in the book – maybe to the end of this chapter and look at the strategies for dealing with flashbacks and triggers. Later talk with a supporter about your difficulties with this chapter.)

Starting therapy with John
The story in the book isn't going to make sense unless I go back to the beginning of therapy with John following my collapse when working with the bullying head teacher.

I knew from things my colleagues at school told me that she was 'setting me up' and manipulating situations. I found her behaviour intimidating and I became terrified of her – conflict like this was not something I could deal with easily.

Initially, therapy with John was to help me to deal with the situation at school. With him I began to understand about my low self-esteem. I hadn't realized how much I believed my mother's words, 'You are hopeless' and 'You will never come to anything', and her sense that her unhappiness was all my fault.

It felt magical that after two years with John, sitting clutching my Eeyore, I began to like myself a bit. I could even look at myself in a mirror. I saw how my mother had manipulated me, and how she had put the family stress onto me rather than taking some of the responsibility for it herself.

So now when the head teacher was putting all the ills in the school onto me and not taking responsibility for the things that were going wrong because of her irrational behaviour, I was back to being a powerless child again – the scapegoat.

I began to see things more clearly. I wasn't an evil person. It wouldn't be better if I was dead. I wasn't ugly, hopeless and useless. I didn't really know what low self-esteem was when I started working with John, but after two years I was smiling at myself and that astonished me.

Although I couldn't understand how that change took place in me, it was so good to feel it.

But during the last few months of the therapy, the images in my mind became scarier. I was again having nightmares most nights and although they still included the head teacher, there were new elements to them that I couldn't understand.

John suggested that I try to write down some of my dreams and this was helpful and gave us both insights into my inner thoughts.

But mostly I didn't want to think about these images. Sometimes these were flashbacks (sudden and unexpected mental images during the day), and this was something new for me – and terrifying. I began to wonder if I was going mad.

I became suicidal again.

For a few months I felt completely trapped by these images and as soon as they came into my mind I would 'pull down a blind' to shut them out. But I realized that if I could be brave enough, while I was with John, I could try to see what the images were.

It took me ages to pluck up the courage to do that.

The first image was my step-father's face leering at me over the cot bars. I couldn't understand why that was so very scary – except that he was a violent man. But he was dead. So why was it so terrifying?

I worked at 'looking' at these images over a few months and gradually sank back into depression and chaos.

Images become clearer

The next image to come was startling. It was a huge penis coming into my mouth. My feeding bottle of milk was taken away and the penis was put in instead.

I was horrified. Surely no one ever did that. Surely not?

I squirmed with embarrassment and terror trying to tell John. We sat in silence. I couldn't say it, even holding Eeyore – it was too scary.

But when I did, the world did not come to an end. John didn't reject me or tell me I was lying, though I thought I must be. Where had that image come from? Why did it spin around my brain, shutting out all rational thinking?

I knew with a deep certainty that I must be making it up. (Over the years I lost this certainty and replaced it with a cautious acceptance that 'something happened'. My memories can't give me a totally accurate picture though.)

The Cleveland enquiry

One reason why I was so certain that I was making it all up was that often on the news at that time there was something about an enquiry into the sexual abuse of children in Cleveland.

I knew I was responding oddly to these news items. A peculiar fear would hit me, and at the same time I had a little girl in my class at school whom we thought was being sexually abused by her father. I found meetings about that with social workers and so on very difficult, but didn't know why except that I so much wanted to help this child, but felt so helpless.

I thought that any worries I had about sex (and there were lots of these) were all due to the 'rape' in the park when I was six.

That explained everything, didn't it?

Flashbacks

I didn't know what was happening to me with the flashbacks – these disturbing moments that came suddenly and unpredictably into my life and seemed to be happening in the present. Once I started to tell John about them he assured me I wasn't going mad, but of course I didn't believe everything he said – barrel-loads of humbug-detecting fluid are needed at all times with therapists!

The flashbacks were hideous and terrifying. But looking back on those awful years I can see that flashbacks can teach us something of the truth of what happened in the past.

Those who constantly tell us not to dwell on the past don't understand that flashbacks come of their own accord. They are not things under our control. Like dreams they are there – sudden and unwelcome – and it is better to learn strategies for dealing with them than to listen to our friends declaring how we must 'move on'.

We know that!

If we could, we would. But it takes time to break the chains of abuse.

Strategies for dealing with flashbacks and similar startling triggers

(I'm grateful to the Bristol Crisis Service for Women for help with this section – see the resources section.)

Flashbacks can hit at any time; they seem not to be related to current stress or to what we are doing. I've gone for more than a year without one, thought they were over, and then have been hit hard by an unexpected one. So now I try not to be surprised if another one strikes.

1. Tell yourself you are having a flashback, and this is OK and normal in people who were traumatized as children or adults.

2. Remind yourself that the worst is over – it happened in the past,

but it is not happening now. However bad you feel, you survived the awfulness in the past, which means you can survive what you are remembering now.

3. Call on the 'adult' part of yourself to tell your 'Inner Child' that she/he is not in any danger now and you will get through this together. (More about your Inner Child in chapter nine.)

4. Let your Inner Child know it's OK to remember and to feel like this – indeed it will help you heal from what happened in the past. Your Inner Child is communicating with you the only way she/he knows, SO LISTEN!

5. Try some of these ways of 'grounding' yourself so you become more aware of the present:

❖ Stamp your feet and grind them around on the floor to remind yourself where you are now.

❖ Look around yourself, noticing the colours, the people, the shape of things.

❖ Listen to the sounds around you: traffic, voices, birds singing, the washing machine etc.

❖ Feel your body, the boundary of your skin, your hair, the chair/ground supporting you

❖ Keep an elastic band on your wrist so you can ping it against your skin – the feeling is NOW, the things you are re-experiencing are in the past.

6. Take care of your breathing: breathe deeply down to your diaphragm (belly breathing). Put your hand just above your navel and breathe so that your hand gets pushed up and down, and count to five each time you breathe in, and again as you breathe out, slowing your breathing down. (When we get scared we breathe too quickly and shallowly and our body begins to panic because we are not getting enough oxygen. This causes dizziness, shakiness and more panic. We stop the panic by breathing deeply and slowly.)

7. If you've lost a sense of where you end and the rest of the world begins, rub your body so you can feel its edges and the boundary of you. Wrap yourself in a blanket and feel it around you.

8. Get support if you would like it. Let people close to you know about the flashbacks so they can help if you want them to. That might mean holding you, talking to you, helping you to reconnect with the present and reminding you that you are safe and cared for now.

9. Flashbacks are powerful experiences that drain your energy, so take time to look after yourself. You could have a warm bath, or have a sleep under your duvet with some of your creatures. Your Inner Child and you deserve to be taken care of, given all that you went through in the past.

10. When you feel ready, write down all you can remember about the flashback and how you got through it. This will help you to remember information for your healing and remind you that you did get through it (and can again).

11. If you have problems believing the abuse happened, remind yourself that you now have another bit of 'evidence' that 'something happened'. (Presumably the flashback memory may not be an exact replication of what happened, but it will contain some truth.)

12. Remember you are not crazy – flashbacks are normal. And YOU ARE HEALING!

KEY POINTS

■ Hidden memories are likely to emerge anyway, in nightmares and flashbacks, so it is wise to listen to them rather than squashing them down again.

■ Thinking that we have made it up is a problem for all survivors who do not have total recall of what happened in the past.

■ Inventing abuse is rare.

■ Memories of abuse can emerge many years after the actual event and won't always give us a totally accurate picture of what happened.

■ Triggers for remembering can be varied. (More of this later.)

■ We can teach ourselves strategies for dealing with unpleasant things that happen as our memories come back.

(There is more about memories in chapter thirteen, so if this is a big issue for you you might want to skip on to that chapter.)

CHAIN BREAKING

1. We must take positive action to break the chains that hold us in so much pain. Read the list of strategies for dealing with flashbacks again and focus on the strategies that appeal to you.

2. Try to memorize some strategies so that you can use them when a flashback strikes. (I used to write things on little bits of card and take them with me when I went out so that if I started to freak out I'd read the card and use that to calm myself down.)

3. In your drawing book or journal, draw or write about good things you have already done. Focusing on our achievements helps us to be more positive and to achieve more.

4. My friend Judy suggested that we draw our flashbacks. As she said this we both burst out laughing because we both had the same thought. 'Now I've got teeth!' (Wasn't it Freud who talked about biting a penis off?) I've tried drawing and painting my flashbacks. It can be releasing – and it feels great.

5. If your memories are really hazy as mine are, don't force them, but try to be honest with yourself. Why would you have symptoms such as flashbacks if 'nothing happened'? As one doctor said to me, you might well get all the symptoms of abuse even if there was just one event of any kind of abuse – maybe even abuse that some people might call 'mild'.

6. Even if you are too unsure to acknowledge the abuse, you can decide to do something to change your life for the better. Think of something small and achievable that you could do. For example, I decided to stop gnawing my fingers and drawing blood every day. First I worked out the times when I chewed badly (car journeys) and with gritted teeth decided I had to change. With a combination of foul-

tasting stuff to paint on my nails and nagging myself, over a couple of years I stopped doing it. (Mostly!)

(Make sure when you decide to change something that it is something you have the power to change: you can't change other people.)

Remember

Flashbacks can help break a chain so write/draw/think/speak/dance them.

Love is essential to brain development in the early years of life... and...
early interactions between babies and their parents have lasting and serious
consequences.
SUE GERHARDT

5 Abuse and depression

People who have been abused are left with many problems, especially if they are not listened to. When they are unheard, life takes on a sense of frenzied doom with the frantic search for help – and the awful dawning realization that there isn't much help out there.

Nowhere feels safe. Depression, a hideous condition, can overcome us and we sink into our dark hole where we lie alone.

- There is nowhere to cry.

- We're too afraid to reach out.

- We feel like some alien who doesn't belong in this world.

- We feel abandoned and rejected.

- Our lives will never be the same again.

Depression is everywhere
Depression will apparently hit one in four or five of us at some stage in our life – some say it is even more common than that. Depression can hit anyone, in any social circumstances, at any time, and it is always devastating.

I'm not talking here about just being a bit 'down' or 'blue' – mood swings that affect everyone. I'm meaning full-blown 'I-cannot-cope-at-all-with-life-and-death-seems-quite-attractive' thinking that affects us so severely that we crumple under the strain.

It makes sense to me that if we have been abused, our body can quite reasonably retreat into depression. I think that is our body trying to cope, but also our body is screaming at us to take some action to reduce the stress in our innermost self.

Major life damage
Some abused people have just one depressed episode but others have repeated bouts of depression. The fall-out from this repeated depression can significantly affect our lives, and on top of the trauma from the abuse we are now talking major life damage.

• The depressed feelings that we are hopeless and worthless can tend to make us less likely to want to aim high at a really good education and career.

• Any feelings of low self-esteem we picked up through the abuse are now magnified.

• Depression can tend to make us want to withdraw from life ('They won't want gloomy me along with them on their fun night out').

• We don't keep up with relationships (apathy can take over in depression so friends can drift away).

• If making any kind of commitment to someone is scary because of our loss of trust in people resulting from abuse, making strong relationships becomes almost impossible and we may just want to be left alone in our dark, isolated pit.

• If we find holding down a job difficult when we are depressed, this can make future employment problematic. Some people spend many years trying to find a job, but as time goes on, some survivors say their low self-esteem gets even worse with all the rejections, and they can become bitter and resentful at the prejudice in society towards people with mental distress and other problems.

• We may tend to lean too much on other people, and this can lead to all kinds of relationship problems. Clingy demanding people can be a real turn-off both at work and at home.

• Depressed people tend to feel physical pain more deeply, so we might sink into illness rather easily.

• Depressed people tend to ruminate about things, so all the time we might be playing our 'old tapes' over and over in our mind. 'I'm such a bad person. I deserve to have an awful life like this.'

This kind of negative thinking pushes us further into depression – it can become too much and we collapse in a heap.

What kind of depression?

No one could put their finger on what was behind my depression. I was profoundly depressed at various stages in my teenage years (but no one then called it depression). When I first left home to go to university I began to be suicidal and looking back on that now I realize that my mother had taught me to believe that I couldn't manage without her. I wanted to get out of home because it was so awful, but once away, I couldn't cope.

Nowhere was safe.

It wasn't until I was married that I was told I suffered from 'endogenous' depression because there seemed to be no reason to be depressed. The doctor was kind and said that, having moved to a new city, just got married, had really bad 'flu and so on, it was to be expected that I would get depressed. (These days I think some doctors might have labelled my depression as 'reactive', meaning it was in reaction to circumstances, or they might have said it was 'post-viral' depression following the 'flu.)

Then I was depressed again shortly after the birth of our son, as we prepared to move to a different town. The move made me anxious, so there seemed to be a reason for that depressed time.

When I had my second baby, I was said to be suffering from post-natal depression – though given that I had been very depressed while I was pregnant with her I was never much convinced by that particular label, although I could see clearly that my emotions were all over the place.

I don't remember much of it but I do remember crying for hours.

Depression and labels

If survivors hide their abuse from their doctors, it could be that they will end up with a diagnosis that isn't quite right. So if we can, it would be best to tell our doctor about the abuse. But if you don't think you can do that, that's OK.

There are loads of different labels for depression, but I'm not sure how much these matter. I've had lots of different labels from the herd of psychiatrists I seem to have run into at various times. Labels seem to help the doctors – once you are labelled they know what to do. So you can use your label to help your recovery; take from it what helps you and dump the rest.

If the doctor thinks we might need some kind of medical intervention they are likely to say we have 'clinical depression'. This seems to mean that doctors think they can treat it. (People I know who have been told by their doctor that their depression isn't 'clinical' can get a bit freaked out about that. So their mood isn't treatable because it isn't bad enough? That is guaranteed to send their mood plummeting to the bottom of their dark pit!)

Whatever label you might be given, it can be helpful to think of depression as an illness to do with an imbalance of chemicals in your brain. But remember that some psychologists, therapists and counsellors don't like the word 'illness' being used for depression and see it not as a chemical imbalance as a doctor might, but purely as warped thinking (see Dorothy Rowe's books in the resources section).

The depression isn't happening because you are bad or pathetic or worthless, though you might feel that very strongly.

Treatment for depression

People get better from depression. Anti-depressants can be very effective. They can lift our mood so that we feel well enough to talk about our feelings. DON'T buy these off the internet though. Go to your doctor. Take their advice.

'Talking treatments' (counselling and therapy) can change our lives and help us in the long term not to hang on to our negative thinking – our 'old tapes' that say, 'I'm such a bad person I deserve this awful illness. I'll never get better. I'm so worthless I don't deserve any help.'

Some people need tranquillizers as well as or instead of anti-depressants because anxiety is often mixed in with the depression. Most survivors have such worrying thoughts that many of us might need both kinds of medication. I need both, although one reason for that is to prevent me from getting too 'high' and rushing around generating dozens of new projects (that I'm unlikely to be able to finish) when I'm not sitting at the bottom of my deep dark cliff face.

Some depressed people find 'alternative therapies', such as homeopathic or herbal remedies work for them. (I find herbal teas calming and they are so much better for us than lots of caffeine.)

Self-help treatments

Recent research shows that having a good diet and taking some exercise are hugely beneficial for depression – that's definitely true in my life. Of course getting out for a brisk walk could be very difficult on days when you are so depressed you don't want to get out of bed. Or if you have mobility problems.

But that walk, or dancing to loud music, or whatever grabs you to raise your pulse rate and get those endorphins rushing around your body, can do wonders.

A simple meal of real food (not processed), will give us the nutrients we need. If you feel so bad you don't want to cook, just go for healthy snacks like fruit, nuts, vegetables, cereal, cheese, eggs and yogurt – *definitely* not junk food, which is full of bad fats, sugar and added chemicals. There is a huge amount of evidence that junk and processed food can make you feel ill, and damage your body. You don't need that on top of the depression and post-traumatic stress from the abuse.

Denying the strength of the pain

If our memories of the abuse are either totally hidden to us, or we are denying the strength of our pain at what happened (because it is much easier and more pleasant to say 'it was nothing' than it is to admit to our furious outrage, shame, guilt etc.), then we may not link our depression (or burnout, panic attacks, phobias, high blood pressure or tension headaches etc.) to abuse. It is all violently boiling away silently inside us but we cannot give words to what we are feeling, so it is hardly surprising that well-meaning psychiatrists and others are perplexed. Here is another patient for whom there seems no clear reason for his or her depression.

What could be going on is that our brain refuses to think the unthinkable, so instead the unthinkable comes out in a different way, such as depression, or self-harming, or eating disorders, or Obsessive Compulsive Disorder.

Survivors and depression

It is possible that for some people who are depressed or who are repeatedly becoming depressed and where it is hard to detect the real cause, there might be some traumatic abuse at the back of it all.

I'm not saying that all depressed people were sexually abused. Not at all. But if we think of the other kinds of abuse – physical, emotional, verbal, childhood neglect, abandonment, and bullying at school and work – maybe some kind of abuse can be one of the important factors in many people's depression.

Depression as a defence

The really worrying thing about depression is that it is probably an outward sign of something going on inside us that is so bad we cannot face it. So at some point in our various bouts of depression we have to ask ourselves, 'What is behind the depression?'

The unthinkable thing can be a whole range of different factors, not just earlier abuse:

- our perfectionism
- the pressures put on us by parents
- low self-esteem
- our internal anger that we dare not express or even believe exists

…and so on.

We might be depressed following some difficult event, such as:

- being made redundant
- divorce or having an awkward teenager in the family
- realizing we might never have a child, or get married, or have a partner

…and so on.

These factors combine with the left-over damage from the earlier abuse and can cause us to spiral down into the bleakness of depression that is so very hard to shift.

Depression and loss
Depression is almost always about some sense of loss. For example, the loss of:

- any sense of being safe (which is why we must create a safe place)
- the ability to trust others
- peace of mind
- any sense of self-worth and self-esteem
- a sense of love and security
- a sense of belonging
- any sense of something to look forward to
- any sense of being comfortable in our body.

These have gone and in place of them we have the anxiety and fear, the nightmares and intrusive thoughts, and such a sense of guilt and worthlessness that our lives will never be the same again.

We must learn to grieve for what we have lost, and allow ourselves to feel anger at what was done to us.

Depression shines a light

Depression forces us to face life full-on and ask ourselves the most basic of questions.

1. 'What is life really about?'

2. 'Do I want to be alive?'

3. 'Is there a God? (Because if there is, where was he when I was being abused?')

4. 'How do I find fulfilment in life?'

The depression signals to us that something is wrong and if we can read those signals and make a promise to ourselves to turn our life around – slowly and with great effort – then we can break those chains that hold us down.

That is hard, but if I can do it, so can you!

Strategies for getting better from depression

1. Remember always to be kind to yourself. Eat well and go for walks.

2. Make achievable lists to prevent too much procrastinating. (I'm a world champion procrastinator and list maker.) Always put onto the list something you've already done so you can check it off straight away.

3. Join a self-help group (see the resources section at the back).

4. Create a 'safety net' for the worst days, such as a 'special box' by your bed in which you keep cards and letters that mean positive things for you, photos and so on of the good times. Dip into the box at the worst moments.

5. Treat yourself kindly.

Treating yourself kindly means looking after yourself. Yet this is the one thing you will not do. If you were physically ill and not depressed at the same time, you would look after yourself… but here you are, enduring one of the most punishing experiences a body can take, and you do nothing to help your body to cope. Worse than that, you do the opposite. Instead of resting, you push yourself to do more and more. When you do lie down to rest, instead of thinking of pleasant things or indulging in a delightful fantasy, you lie there thinking of horrible things and imagining the worst.

DOROTHY ROWE

Strategies for getting rid of negative thinking

1. One of the most significant things we can do for ourselves is to challenge our negative thinking – those 'old tapes' ('I'm no good at anything') – and replace them with more positive thinking ('I'm reading this book and I'm going to get good at chain breaking').

2. If we work on this, we can detect those things that we say to ourselves that are keeping us in unhappiness. 'It was all my fault' is a common thing we say, and that thought sometimes seems so locked into us that we cannot break it. (This is something this book touches on a few times.) We can become experts at putting ourselves down, and this is keeping us depressed.

3. Quite a large part of our negative thinking can be closely linked to our low self-esteem. (There is more of that later in the book.)

4. The next time you decide you don't have the energy to do something, such as go out with your mates, challenge yourself. How much do I not want to go? I hate the whole idea! But make yourself go out, then when you are back ask yourself if you enjoyed it. When I do this I find that my anticipated hatred of going out, or meeting someone, isn't true to the actual, much more positive, feeling when I do!

KEY POINTS

■ Depression is very common and is likely to hit survivors in response to the trauma they faced.

■ Labels from doctors aren't always relevant but we can use the label to understand more about ourselves and our healing.

- A good diet and some exercise each day is important throughout life and can help depression to lift.

- Depression is almost always about some kind of loss.

- We need to learn to deal with our negative thinking.

CHAIN BREAKING

1. One effective way to 'listen' to ourselves is to find someone to talk to whom we trust.

2. If you think you are depressed it is important to go to your doctor.

3. Try to think back over the past few days. Do you listen too much to your 'old tapes' (things from the past that go round and round in your mind)? Write about this or draw a picture. You could make some 'positive tapes' for yourself to play back when you need nurturing, such as favourite music or the sounds whales make.

4. Depression is often about the loss of something important in our lives. Look back at the examples of loss above on page 48. Try to list things you lost.
   It's good to feel angry about those losses – that shows you are *feeling*.
   In fact it is crucial that you let yourself feel the sadness of what you lost. There is usually grieving to do in depression.

5. How is your plan working out for reading this book? Write or draw a bit about how you are feeling about your 'uncovery'. *I'm uncovering...*

6. Is your safe place working out? If not, how can you change it?

7. Have you got yourself an Eeyore or a cuddly bear? Charity shops sometimes have creatures sitting waiting to be loved and needed.

Remember
Recovery from trauma needs time.
   Nurture yourself rather than 'beating yourself up'.
   You only need to be 'goodenough'. You don't need to be perfect.

What I am is good enough if I would only be it openly.
CARL ROGERS

6 The emergency stage

I deliberately didn't put this chapter about what some people call the 'emergency stage' at the start of the book because for many survivors, this worst bit can happen quite a long time after the actual abusive event.

The emergency stage is the time when:

- we can no longer hold down our 'hidden memories'

- we're on 'red alert'

- nightmares and night terrors seem out of control

- our emotions are all over the place and mood swings – from rage to deep sadness – are common.

What's happening is that now we've done some 'uncovery' and a little 'discovery', the full extent of our hurt can hit us and that can be devastating. We've 'discovered' things that we can hardly believe.

Adult rape and domestic violence victims sometimes remember what happened vividly, and after the initial rage and confusion they can find that, instead of the feelings getting better, the emotional upset grows rather than diminishes.

- There might be a trial to get through. (They know this will be traumatic, partly because in some countries, including Britain, despite many rape cases being taken to court, the chance of getting a conviction is slim.)

- Somehow life has to be put back together again.

- Normal life seems impossible.

But it is important to remember that we are unlikely to recover properly unless we give ourselves this time to uncover and discover.

Memories triggered

A whole range of things can trigger our memories:

- maybe some kind of gut feeling

- a smell (many survivors talk of the huge impact of smell on memory)

- other senses: taste, hearing, touch, sight

- a moment in a film

- looking at a photo

- meeting someone you haven't met for years

- a big life event such as changing jobs

- hearing someone talking about abuse, and so on.

There must be hundreds of different triggers depending on our unique abuse situations.

It can be really important to understand our triggers so that we can learn to cope with them – and learn to predict when they will come.

Listening to our body

Although we must find ways to cut off from the pain when we are triggered and somehow get on with life, we must also listen and learn from triggers. Our body is screaming at us to listen and to take notice of those feelings we have been trying to repress.

We have to stop minimizing the effects of the abuse if we are to start to break those chains that hold us in the fear and nightmares.

We've been saying to ourselves for too long, 'It was nothing. I'm fine. I can handle this.'

It was serious, we are not fine and we cannot handle it on our own because the inner pain is too great.

The kinds of things that can be happening at the emergency stage were listed briefly in chapter three and this is a little more detail about them.

- Flashbacks (see chapter four).

- Disturbing/racing thoughts – these can be upsetting and add to our panic.

- Panic attacks – times when we can have a range of symptoms from feeling we can't breathe to a pounding heart. If it feels as if the panic goes on all day (as mine often did) this is called an 'anxiety state'.

(See the strategies for dealing with panic and anxiety at the end of chapter three.)

• Difficulties when our level of fear becomes overwhelming.

• Compulsions – these can be very varied and can be so bad that we end up with Obsessive Compulsive Disorder. This can be mild (checking we've locked the door when we go out – once is OK, more than that and we need to think carefully about what is going on), or it can be so bad that 'normal' life is impossible, for example, washing our hands fifty times in a morning or eating when we are not hungry – maybe compulsively eating all the time resulting in immobility, loss of a job and so on.

• Difficulties in communicating to people how we are feeling. We might try to cover up our feelings at home or work, but the creeping depression and exhaustion from poor sleep can make us inefficient. When asked 'Are you OK?', we know it is best not to launch into talking about the abuse. People can be deeply shocked and unable to cope if we tell the truth of what happened and the possibility that we will end up feeling rejected is so high it is best to keep quiet. (Anyway, in western culture most people expect us to say we are 'fine' when they ask us how we are! Even if they know we aren't OK. So it is best just to say that we're 'fine'.)

• Raw and angry emotions can make us irritable even with those we love and outbursts of anger are likely to happen.

• We might find we cannot cope with a sexual relationship that we used to find comforting. (And if our sexual partner is not able to accept our need for some space and insists on sex whether we like it or not, for some survivors this can mean nightmares now happen when they are awake as well.)

• We might find we can't concentrate for more than a few seconds, so reading or going to work can be difficult.

• Some find they cannot even watch a video if there is even the slightest hint of sex in it.

• We might be having sleep difficulties – problems with getting to sleep, nightmares, night screaming and so on – and become exhausted, baggy-eyed and afraid to go to sleep, resulting in our family feeling helpless.

- Some have other health difficulties.

- Self-harming can start or get worse as a way of coping.

- Suicidal thoughts can become a problem again.

- We are likely to feel we are going mad, but we're not – this is Post-Traumatic Stress Disorder.

- We might be 'freaking out' or 'spacing out' quite a lot of the time.

It is not uncommon for the psychiatric and other caring services to say that they cannot help us.

1. The rape crisis centre may be too full to give us a place.

2. The anti-depressants may not suit us and we may hate the feeling of being drugged and turned into a zombie – the loss of control can feel terrifying.

3. The community psychiatric nurse may not always have time for us (or we might not want that kind of help anyway. It filled me with horror to have someone visit me every Wednesday at 2pm!).

4. Some of the help may be withdrawn until we stop habits like self-injury or refusing to eat.

5. We might be given odd labels such as 'borderline personality' – and if you've been given that label you'll know what I mean by the scathing tone some doctors can use. It seems to me from my reading that doctors don't know what to do with some survivors, so they dump them into a bin called 'borderline'.

6. Some of the 'help' can be completely inappropriate where there is no real understanding of the time it can take to recover from abuse and little understanding of features of recovering from trauma such as depression ('Pull yourself together').

7. Counselling may not be available for another six months, or the help available is so expensive that we cannot afford it.

…and so on. So we can end up having to find our own way through it all.
    No wonder survivors love their cuddly teddies!

Lack of understanding

When people don't understand the profound effects of sexual abuse, the help on offer can be ineffective and at worst it can increase the pain of the abused person. It can make them feel they are beyond help (which is terrifying), guilty at taking up so much time yet not getting better despite months of help, ashamed ('I told you all that and now I wish I hadn't') and worried that they are not worthy of help.

Often abused people find that talking to their family or friends about the abuse can cause great upset in the family or community.

This can result in:

• rejection by the family or community. This can get so bad that abused people are told, 'We never want to see you again. You don't belong in this family until you take back your allegations.'

• splitting of the family or community. This can happen when one section stands by the abused person. This can have far-reaching effects and blame may land on survivors!

• children being profoundly affected and in rare cases removed from an abused parent on the grounds that the parent might abuse them, or that the parent is so upset that their life falls apart for a while.

Some need to escape

The combination of the emergence of these deep feelings and the shame, rejection and overwhelming sense of guilt and desolation makes this a time of profound personal trauma (again). For some, the shame is so great that they feel rejected and so guilty that they hide from people, becoming reclusive. Others decide to leave home and make a new start, but can end up living on the streets of our big cities. This includes quite young children escaping from abuse at home, at school or in another community.

My emergency stage went on and off for several years. Not every day was as bad as some.

My blood pressure soared.

I went for distraction as my main survival strategy, so I worked very hard.

I relaxed by watching videos over and over again. (My favourite was *Independence Day*, in which Bill Pullman saves the world from ugly monsters who want to take over the universe. Very appropriate.)

I slept on the sofa downstairs with videos playing all night so that all my horrible thoughts were drowned by sound and action on the screen.

I managed to make meals and get out to the gym and the shops but only survived that by having lots of time on my own.

Sometimes I read a few sentences in *The courage to heal work book* (see resources section) and wrote a few comments, but mostly this work book freaked me out, although at times it was comforting to realize I was not alone in what I was feeling.

It all gets too much

Some people cope with this high level of anxiety by not coping. So they get taken into hospital – but when there they may not tell anyone about the abuse. This might seem odd, but it can be hugely demanding to talk about what happened. Even thinking of telling kindly friends can make us feel too vulnerable to cope, so we stay silent.

During my times in mental hospitals (several before I worked with John but only once since then), it was most marked that patients would tell each other about the abuse but wouldn't tell the doctors. Some were still being abused. But still nothing was said and looking back now on my own admissions to hospitals, sometimes after suicide attempts, as far as I can remember the subject of my 'rape' by a stranger at age six and the molestations by my older brother (which I could remember – it was the sexual abuse by my step-father that I had 'forgotten') were never mentioned (I suppose because no one ever asked me questions about these incidents).

Sexual abuse just wasn't talked about then. Anyway, you'd have to trust a doctor to tell them that kind of thing and trust was not on my agenda while in hospital.

Some survivors find friends who can help, or a church family where they are accepted and loved, or a group of other abused people who can provide a place of peace or at least some sense that they are not struggling through this terrible phase on their own.

Are you a ruminator?

It seems that the world is divided into ruminators and non-ruminators. I'm definitely a ruminator and I can go over and over something negative in my mind – worrying, and getting my level of panic and anxiety up so far that I can feel ill. I have this theory that the more I think about something, the more likely it is that I will solve the problem and it will go away!

Of course, that is nonsense.

The reverse is happening: the more I think about it the worse it is getting inside me.

(Of course, 'reflecting' on something positive and thinking through ways to learn from our lives and move on is quite different from this negative ruminating. Reflection can make us feel empowered as we seek for ways to find contentment in life.)

Some positive thoughts

1. It might sound as if this emergency stage is all pain and horror, but something positive is going on – we have had a major breakthrough. We are starting to 'uncover' our emotions and are becoming aware of the extent of those emotions within us – admitting it hurts – and this is the place where we all need to start.

2. This can be the time at which we are being the most honest with ourselves about our past life, and we need to stick with those feelings and tell ourselves that now we know more of the truth, we can begin to heal.

3. Remember that kindness and tenderness is out there for us to find, sometimes in unexpected places. My new little Annie-dog became ill when she was only a year old, and although the local people said the vet could be 'surly and difficult', I found his all-out efforts to save Annie shone a light into the bleakness of my struggles. I'd raged at God to leave me my precious little puppy. 'Please don't take her,' I begged over several days. But Annie had to be put to sleep and I felt I would die from my sadness. I decided to find a teddy to represent the kindness of the vet, and as I cuddle MacAllister now, he reminds me that love is out there for us.

Strategies for surviving the emergency stage

Hopefully this book will help you through this emergency stage when feelings are raw and violent, and when it can feel that the rest of your life is going to be this hell on earth.

1. The most crucial thing to remember in this horrible stage is that it will end.

2. Be kind to yourself.

3. Nurture yourself by doing something you like, such as a hobby, or treating yourself to something such as a visit to a charity shop to buy some new clothes.

4. The world can go on without you for a bit, so try to take 'time out'.

5. Retreat to your bed or wherever you feel safe. (You MUST have a safe space – this is top priority.)

6. Cuddle your favourite toy.

7. Remember that you might not be the best student on the course, the best friend to your mates, the best cook, parent, secretary or whatever, but almost certainly you are a 'goodenough' student, friend, father etc.

8. Distract yourself in some way. (OK, I know as a long-term strategy that's not ideal, but when the chains are strangling us and we feel traumatized and desperate, distraction is great – because it works.)

9. Dip in and out of this book as your moods take you, remembering you can only do so much, then you must rest.

KEY POINTS

■ The emergency stage is awful. It is likely to be the worst time of your life after the abuse, but it will end.

■ Triggers that bring back memories are varied and common, and are likely to go on for ages, sometimes years.

■ We are starting to 'uncover' our emotions – and that is the start of the healing process.

■ There are strategies we can use to get ourselves through this stage.

■ We must be kind to ourselves. Nothing is gained by beating ourselves up about difficult issues, such as feeling we 'must' forgive.

CHAIN BREAKING

1. Make good use of your safe place. This can be a real place and/or a place in your mind that you can escape into. I have both.

2. Try to write a little about what triggers your memories. A smell? Certain words? (For me, one glimpse of someone jiggling their leg up and down and I had to escape – but I'm much better than I was.)

3. If you haven't already, start a journal. This can be the way to understand what has happened and once we understand, we can start to put our lives back together again.

4. If you haven't already done it, make yourself a list of emergency contacts.

5. You might want to write yourself some notes and stick them up around the house, for example:
All of these difficult things are normal after abuse.
I'm not going mad.
It wasn't my fault.
It will get better!

6. Try to draw or paint your feelings. No one is going to see it so go for it – big brushes are great on big paper and you can stab and stir as violently as you like.

7. If you find you are going over and over things in your mind, make a list of your worries. Write as much as you can about them, then make a conscious decision to put them aside by doing something creative and nurturing for yourself.

8. Don't worry about people telling you you 'must' forgive. However much they nag you, it is an unnecessary worry at this stage and will only make you feel more guilty, which is likely to overburden you to the point of collapse. Forgiveness is more appropriate once you've uncovered and discovered a bit more.

Remember

You are not going mad.
  These feelings will go away.

> *Undeserved guilt may have nothing at all to do with our harming someone else, but it has everything to do with **believing** that we did. Emotional blackmailers encourage us to take global responsibility for their complaints and unhappiness, doing all they can to reprogram the basic and necessary mechanisms of appropriate guilt into the undeserved guilt production line where the lights continually flash guilty, guilty, guilty.*

SUSAN FORWARD

Suzie-doll

Part 2

Deciding to heal

This section is about making a decision to get better and to break our chains. As we try to struggle free from the awfulness of the emergency stage, we realize that there are many more chains than we thought there were. The flashbacks and nightmares seem to go on forever, but as we uncover more of our feelings, so we discover that it is we who must make the decision to heal for ourselves.

This section has some practical strategies for making that happen.

Even if you're on the right track, you'll get run over if you just stand there.

WILL ROGERS

7 Images, dreams and reality

You might think that 'deciding' to heal doesn't sound quite right for this section, but it is a choice we need to make at some point.

It's no good sitting around waiting for a better quality of life just to arrive in our lap. We do need to make a specific decision that we are going to work at our healing. This can be one of those 'sitting on the end of the bed' transforming moments, as I will call them.

'Do I want to be like this for the rest of my life?'

No.

'So what can I do about that today?'

Transforming moments

One of the themes of this book is the importance of 'transforming moments' in our lives – times when we make big decisions, or times when we make a huge leap forward in our healing.

A few months ago, one of my favourite writers and actors, Victoria Wood, did two brilliant programmes about dieting and the diet industry. At one point she is talking to Sarah, the Duchess of York (who had lost loads of weight), and Victoria asks Sarah how she was able to get rid of her bulges.

Sarah says she sat on the end of her bed one day and asked herself if she was going to be fat for the rest of her life. Did she want that? No. Well, she needed to do something about it, now.

Yes. I know about these 'sitting on the end of the bed' moments, these enormous decisions that we must make if we are to recover from anything, or change our life in any way – recovery from abuse included.

We have to make big decisions that will transform the course of our lives.

Writing down dreams

My life was spiralling out of control, so when John suggested I write down my dreams and nightmares, although at first I thought that very silly, at least it was a place to start in my healing.

The first time I managed to write down a dream before I forgot it, I found it did help – but it was also a bit scary.

At the end of this chapter there are some practical strategies for writing down dreams, but if you feel unsure of this as a way of healing, you might want to talk to one of your supporters about it first – if you have one. I think if you write dreams down and you don't have outside support, it could get overwhelming. If you are also getting many flashbacks at the moment, you could leave the dreams for a few weeks or months.

Take care; there are some potential triggering aspects to this chapter. You might want to be in a safe space before you read on.

Shark attack

Among the most significant of the dreams I talked about with John was a recurring one I had after I watched a programme on television about life under the ocean. It showed how divers take their cameras down in a cage to film sharks, and I wasn't at all aware of this meaning anything particularly significant to me.

The dream happened on several nights during the phase in which the memory of the penis coming through the cot bars was piercing my mind. I kept feeling very sick with this racing memory and remained convinced I had made it up. (Why or how I would do that I don't know.)

After a few attempts I managed to remember enough of the dream to write it down.

I'm in a cage under water. It is all blue and there are fish and some sharks. I'm feeling safe because I am in the cage. The boat is above me. The fish swim away because of the shark. Then the shark comes towards me, but I feel safe – it can't get me. But suddenly it can get through the bars of the cage. It puts its head through and its jaws open wide. Big teeth come towards me. The shark gets right through the bars – coming towards me. I wake up terrified.

'What do you make of that, Sue?' John says.

I sit silently.

The second time I see John that week I tell him I had the dream again. He never pushes me into anything (for which I was hugely grateful, otherwise my worry that I was 'making it all up' would have been even worse than it was).

'The penis coming through the cot bars,' I whisper. If I say it softly it will be easier to take it back. Easier to hide it. Easier to brush it off.

I want to scream and cry and rage. But I do none of those things. I just sit with John, hugging Eeyore, feeling the most evil person on the planet – and deeply convinced that John will send me away, or he will die.

No amount of telling myself to be logical and rational about it seemed to work. The problem with being a person who believed that thinking things through would result in coming to some kind of deeper understanding of something (because of all the hours thinking about it) was that this kind of rational internal debate with myself was not working at all. Why wouldn't my way of living and thinking work any more?

More images emerge

As well as the dreams, more images were intruding into my mind during this time. I finally plucked up the courage to tell John that one aspect of these images was that I could feel intense pain in my body, but I didn't know where that pain was.

This was, I thought, totally loopy! How could I possibly feel pain and not know where it was in my body?

I deeply regretted telling John about the pain because I thought it clearly demonstrated that I was making it up.

I think the pain came along with the flashbacks, but by this time I had a way of disconnecting from flashbacks by 'spacing out' – leaving my body and standing outside myself. Everyone does this to some extent, but I was perfecting it as an art form. It shut down everything, feelings, memories, pain – the whole lot. Wonderful for a short-term coping strategy!

On the ship

The second very significant dream was also a recurring dream, and I sometimes still have it, think about it, wonder about it – and feel so nauseous I want to throw up.

I'm on board a huge ship – a liner with lots of people on it. I'm watching the sea birds, the sun is shining and the sea is a beautiful green with white topped waves. Then Ernie (my step-father) comes up behind me. He leans into me and I can feel his penis. I'm gripping onto the rail. He pushes his penis into my bottom. He puts his hands around my face, over my mouth and I can't breathe.

I jump into the water to get away from him. It's stormy and the wake of the boat almost drowns me.

David is standing at the back of the boat and I wave to him, screaming. I'm drowning and David can't see me or hear me. The boat is disappearing and I know I'm going to drown.

Then I'm in a street. I just have my cloth (a white nappy that I clung to as a child) and I'm throwing up. All this white stuff is pouring out of my mouth. It won't stop. It goes on and on pouring out and I'm choking. No one can help me and it goes on and on, all the white stuff pouring out of me. The white stuff is so deep I'm wading in it.

I try to scream but I can't and I wake up. I still feel sick.

Understanding the pain

I worked out that if we are going to heal we need to realize what our pain means, so I need to leap forward several years in the story now to show how I gradually began to piece together different memories and stick them onto bits of my life that I *could* remember to make some sense of the memories.

The dream on the boat was pretty obvious. It was anal rape. But had that really happened or had I made it up? ('Why would you make it up, Sue?' Ruth, the next therapist I went to, would say. 'Because I'm utterly wicked', I would think. 'Surely you've worked that out by now.')

Over the years I put together things that could relate to that dream, and the mystery pain I felt.

I had begun to sleep in my own bed in my own room as the memories emerged, because of such intense fear of being near people, even David. (Maybe I should say 'especially David because we have a sexual relationship' – and that terrified me at this time of so many phobias.) He had post-viral fatigue syndrome and he was hot and sweaty at night, and I couldn't bear the clamminess of his body – sometimes I couldn't even hold his hand when we were out together. We both found this upsetting, but we agreed to sleep separately.

Despite this I would get searing pains in my bottom during sleep or in the early hours in half sleep. The pains would come with a conviction that a penis was coming into me from behind and I would wake in terror.

But that wasn't happening.

The searing pain and the image of the penis coming into me kept on happening. I hated this and dreaded it. I would leap out of bed and get up, even if it was ridiculously early.

I would go downstairs, make hot chocolate and sit and weep in the kitchen with Jemma-dog and Eeyore.

The body remembers
Right through my time with Ruth I would get this same awful pain – and still do occasionally. And the sense I make of it now?

As a child I had the most terrible constipation. I had tummy pains most of the time and my mother got very worked up about it. I don't think I was all that bothered.

When I was fifteen and looking for any excuse to get out of school (I realize now I was depressed but didn't know that at the time), I decided it was time to make a huge fuss about these pains to get some time off school. I had my appendix taken out – but of course it was healthy so the doctors set about finding out what the pain could possibly be.

I listened carefully to what they said as they stood around my bed and did awful internal examinations.

'… Huge rectum… enormous size…'

At the time this meant nothing to me, but in the last few years I have wondered if these physical symptoms would arise after anal rape? It would make sense.

Many years later, when both my children were very small, I had such bad tummy pain that my doctor in Birmingham sent me off to see a consultant.

He prodded and thought, questioned and was puzzled. Eventually he said very gently to me, 'At some time you have been traumatized and the nervous system controlling your digestion has broken down.' He talked about the water going into the intestine at the wrong place and coming out at the wrong place, and said that I would need to be on medication for the rest of my life.

I wasn't sure about what to make of the 'trauma'. It could have been the time my step-father tried to kill my mother – that was pretty traumatic.

But over the years I wondered if the trauma happened earlier than that?

Body over mind

As I began reading books about how our body remembers when our mind can't, I felt huge relief.

Of course it made sense that if I was young enough to have a bottle of milk in my cot I was really young. I would have no words to explain to myself or anyone else what was going on.

So now I have word-free memories – pains in my body. I was a headache queen for years and must have swallowed thousands of painkillers. Then I found an osteopath. She did some gentle manipulation in my mouth when I told her about the penis-in-the-mouth thing, and along with her doing things to my spine, I rarely get headaches now. (The cranial work also helped with my intense fear of dentists.)

My dreams helped me begin to understand my phobias about swallowing and why I felt such fear of being unable to breathe, as if there was someone on top of me.

These 'body memories' along with my nightmares and dreams were strange at the time, but in the end they were healing.

That emotions are connected in some way to the body should come as no surprise. Everyday speech is full of phrases – in many languages – that reflect the link of emotion and body, psyche and soma. Here are a few examples from American English.

Anger – He's a pain in the neck.
Sadness – I'm all choked up.
Disgust – She makes me sick.
Happiness – I could burst!
Fear – I have butterflies in my stomach.
Shame – I can't look you in the eye.

BABETTE ROTHSCHILD

Piecing together what happened

Like other survivors, I piece things together when I can in an attempt to work out what happened to make me feel trapped in bundles of chains. But with few clear 'real' memories, I went on feeling bad about 'making it all up' – and that itself became a huge chain trapping me in guilt.

Ruth would often say to me, 'You may never know exactly what happened, Sue.'

I had to learn to live with that and continue to sort things out in dreams, flashbacks, pains, memories, physical facts about my body and so on, to try to get as close as I could to the truth.

The truth mattered so much to me.

If I said I was abused and I wasn't, that made me even more evil. God would reject me.

This was the stage when I found church too awful to go to. It was too loud. There were people behind me. The crowds were too terrifying. And communion was very difficult.

Practical strategies for learning from dreams

1. The crucial thing about writing down dreams is to remember not to switch on a strong light, otherwise your memory gets wiped just like a computer when you press the wrong key. I put a really dim bulb (a night light) into my bedside light, but someone told me recently that she doesn't put on the light at all – she just writes and it comes out OK.

You need a pad of paper and pencil placed exactly where you will be able to pick them up immediately. Just write. Don't try and order anything. Write as fast as you can so you don't forget anything. (You will sometimes forget, but try not to worry about that. You will get lots of information from what you remember.)

2. Later in the day go back to the written dream and add bits that you remember when you read it through, or add notes such as 'this bit about the tree came after the bit about the storm' or whatever. Sequencing dreams is hard – and I'm not sure that it matters all that much if we don't get the right order.

3. Ask yourself, 'What sense can I make of this?' Think of the different things in the dream, maybe the sea, the white foam on the top of the waves, or the shark. What meaning can you put onto them?

If you think all this is a load of tosh, that's fine! Probably some of it is and I'm sure it's healthy to keep our humbug detectors fully functioning throughout our healing.

4. I usually found that after a disturbing dream it was best to get up and walk around for a bit, or read a book, or cuddle Eeyore. You might want to plan a nurturing strategy for those terrors that come in the night.

KEY POINTS

■ Our hidden memories can emerge in a range of different ways.

■ Hidden memories can take many years to emerge fully.

■ Dreams and nightmares can sometimes help to make some sense of our hidden memories; so can body pains and fears.

CHAIN BREAKING

1. Set up your bedroom for writing down (or taping) dreams.

2. In order to heal we must admit to the pain. List your hurts, for example, 'Yes, I was hurt. I get terrible nightmares. I wake screaming etc.' It would be good to share that list of hurts with someone.

3. Looking back on your life can you think of some transforming moments? Big decisions? Moments when you understood something more clearly? You need to record any transforming moments as you go through this book – if you don't write or draw them, they might be forgotten and you might lose a key aspect of your chain breaking.

4. Look back to the start of this chapter. Are you able to make a commitment to heal? (You're reading this book so that is a great start.)

5. Imagine it's your 80th birthday party and someone asks you what are the best things you ever did. What are you going to say? Be creative. Snorkelling over the Great Barrier Reef? Running the London marathon? Cuddling your first grandchild?

6. Make a plan to improve your life. (I do this most holidays and put the list on my notice board.) Making little changes can have a big impact on us, such as deciding to go out for a walk every day, or deciding that someone we see is having a negative impact on our life – so deciding to avoid them might be really important.

7. Where do you want to be in a year's time? So what can you do this week to achieve your goal in a year?

Remember

Our aim is to get our inner life in some kind of order, to understand it and to learn to have power over it – not let it have power over us!

You can change the direction of your life.

It is better being a zombie. Safer. A zombie doesn't have any feelings. It can't be hurt. It doesn't worry whether it's a victim, it doesn't feel guilty every time a rerun of 6th March flashes across its memory. There are so many whys and if onlys. Why didn't I do anything to stop it happening? If only I had been wearing something different. Did I lead them on? Encourage them in some way? What else could I have done to prevent it, other than not be there?

JILL SAWARD

8 Transforming moments

The coming of Suzie-doll was like a sledgehammer coming down on my head. The whole of my world changed and I spent days crying, feeling so bruised and hurt that I had to opt out of everything for a while.

I knew I would never be the same person again – my world had changed forever. Getting Suzie was one of the most important moments in my decision to heal.

Ruth and I were at a delicate stage. I just couldn't accept that my weird 'images', nightmares, flashbacks and so on added up to some kind of early abuse that could have been sexual.

Ruth and I talked several times about how therapists could 'suggest abuse'. Ruth wondered what possible motive they could have.

I have no answer to that, but the more I read about sexual abuse the more I hear of reputable and respected people saying that it is very rare for people to make up claims that they were sexually abused. But if you look on the internet, just about every trail you follow for 'sexual abuse' leads you onto sites that make you think that just about every survivor actually has false memories.

This is scary.

Presumably there are lots of people out there who want survivors to stay silent – who want the world to believe that we are all making it up, to believe that sexual abuse is very rare.

It isn't.

Still in 'uncovery'
The day after I had my first thoughts about Suzie-doll I was still in the 'uncovery' stage as I now understand it. I just didn't know what had happened and I was vehemently insisting (especially to myself) that my step-father had done nothing, and that what my older half-brother and uncle did to me really didn't count as sexual abuse. Even the stranger in the park when I was six hadn't actually penetrated me with his penis.

None of this was sexual abuse I insisted, and Ruth and I sat and stared at each other. I knew I was spacing out and trying not to listen to her. I was feeling an overwhelming sense of guilt and shame.

'I'm a horrible person and I made it all up,' I say.

Ruth looks at me and waits.

'I'll just go and get something,' she says and leaves the room. She's never done that before and I start to panic, but she comes back with the most beautiful doll I've ever seen – and a small, cuddly creature Ruth says is the doll's shadow.

Ruth gives them to me to hold and we talk about the doll for the rest of this session and the next one, and something changes in me. I'm not sure what, but I begin to see that the way forward is to get my own baby doll.

I check to see if I have any money in my account and then go shopping, but it's tough. The dolls aren't quite right, so I get on a train and go to Hamleys in central London.

There I find Suzie. I know as soon as I see her that she is 'me'. She has fair hair though, and that is wrong, but her face is right and so is her hairstyle. She's a toddler more than a baby, definitely a little girl. I look at her and already feel passionate about her – despite the price tag.

How could they?

At home with Suzie I get to know her, and talk to her, but I'm not ready for what happens next.

I start to cry. How could anyone hurt a tiny child?

I hold her and weep, realizing that long ago when I watched the film *Something about Amelia* I had 'seen' and acknowledged to myself that it would actually be possible to abuse a small child sexually.

This thought had been too terrifying to hold on to so I'd buried it. Now the evidence I'd collected over the few years since I'd first watched the film was stacking up. I was having to admit to myself that abuse in very early life was possible. This was a major change in my thinking.

As I wept there was some sense of relief, some sense of terror. What was I admitting to myself?

I realized I mustn't go back to where I was in total confusion, and maybe in what psychologists call 'denial'. Maybe.

I moved into a new era that day – a transforming moment when I admitted to myself that the chains were holding me down, that something real had happened to me.

At least now I could start to break some of them.

Our choice to heal

It is our choice to heal, but of course that healing will usually be slow. We can make a huge difference to our lives by making positive choices to heal.

For example, getting a doll or a puppet might be totally wrong for you, but maybe you have other decisions you could make for your own healing. There are some suggestions in the chain breaking section below.

KEY POINTS

■ A doll can help us to connect with our hurt Inner Child.

■ The 'uncovery' stage can be long and painful.

■ We can make positive decisions that can help us to heal.

Chain breaking

1. Do you need a little 'you' to love and care for? (If you were abused as an adult, you still need to comfort and care for the little child within you who was hurt.) Puppets can be wonderful because they can 'talk' to you (see the resources section). Or what about something else creative – that new poetry book that you've longed for, a box of good quality pastels and a new pad of paper, or a trip to the charity shop to buy some cheap clothes?

2. As well as my special box (see page 49) I have two special shelves beside my bed with things that I want to look at every day: photos of David and my children; pictures of puffins; my favourite fossils and crystals; my wooden cross; a model of a child in the huge hand of God that Ruth gave me; and a candle.

These things are to help me to meditate, and just to 'be' in silence. They remind me of peace and that I am 'held'. However bad it gets, I'm safe.

3. If you find writing hard, you can use other visual methods to record your progress (so you don't forget how far you've come).

Posters are great: big bits of paper that you can use to write yourself a message – maybe 'IT WAS NOT MY FAULT', or 'I'M DECIDING TO HEAL'. Or you can use pictures from magazines to make a collage of how you feel, or about the person you want to be.

4. If you're finding working through this book a bit overwhelming, you need to go slower and just take on one idea at a time. I often use a 'word wall' when I need to focus. I write up just one word or one

idea and put it where I can see it. One of my most successful word walls was when I was aware of how anxious and fearful I was and I wrote up 'peace'. I spent a year thinking about how I could make my life less fraught and more peaceful.

5. If you were abused as a child you could make a scrap book to redeem your childhood. Mine has photos from childhood, some of my writing, and also cards and letters that have come to me during the time I've been recovering my memories. This book is about me choosing to heal from those awful years when I was young – I want to grow away from it all and focus instead on the love and care around me now.

You could include in your scrap book ideas about the person you want to become.

Remember
Unless we make a decision to break our chains, we are likely to stay locked into depression, anger, self-blame and poor relationships.

> *I was once told that if people talk about child sexual abuse around children then the youth will lose their innocence. It infuriates me that certain people don't seem to understand that by not talking about things like sexual abuse around children, we are teaching them that it's not OK to talk about it! Surely it's the act of abuse and the imprisonment of silence that causes our youth to 'lose their innocence', not to mention losing their integrity and losing their childhoods.*
>
> HELEN MUNT

9 Making friends with our Inner Child
• • • • • • • • • • • • • • • •

My next decision to heal was to buy Lucia Capacchione's book *Recovery of Your Inner Child* on a whim in a bookshop. It looked like exactly what I needed. I felt so stuck, so bogged down in the mess of all of 'it' – the confusion, the chaos and din in my mind that would never shut up.

Now I had Suzie-doll my life was different because I was more willing to accept that 'something happened', and I went looking for ways to heal. I'd been working through some of *The Courage to Heal*, but I was frustrated with what felt like a tedious process. I wanted to be better *now*, and ditch all that junk about early sexual abuse and move on.

More 'uncovery' and 'discovery'

Looking back on this time I can see that I still had lots to 'uncover' from the depths of myself, and as I read Lucia's book I was excited by her idea that I was quite 'normal' because it isn't just those abused in childhood whose Inner Child has gone into hiding. She says that everyone tends to hide their Vulnerable Self and it is releasing that Feeling Self – the part of us that is spontaneous, enthusiastic and creative – that can heal us.

I was a little nervous of this because of my deep hatred of myself when I get 'high' and go into spontaneous and impetuous mode. (I make all kinds of mistakes that I regret afterwards and added to that I have developed a conviction that David also hates me when I am like that – though he says he doesn't!)

So although Lucia suggests that we do Inner Child work with some kind of support or sharing, I thought it was an activity that I would do secretly on my own.

Become like a little child

One major attraction of letting myself find my Inner Child was that I am always a child in my dream world – where I feel safe, myself, nurtured and loved. Added to that I remembered with some shame that John had commented that I clearly didn't want to grow up.

No. I didn't. I find the adult world horrific. It is full of fear, and many people have that weird way of valuing money, status and power above things like family, love and friendship.

I would rather play hide and seek than read a newspaper and I like children's literature better than adults'. Added to that, my great hero, the man Jesus, said that we would only enter into the kingdom of God (which probably means lots of different things such as finding some spiritual peace through trusting in the unconditional love of God) if we became like a little child.

So becoming like a little child and entering into that world seemed an excellent idea to me.

Finding your Inner Child

The basic way to start to find your Inner Child is to find a quiet place where you will be able to concentrate for a few minutes. Gather together pens, pencils, paper or your journal, and anything else you need – I like to have Suzie-doll with me, or a creature to suit my mood.

Then start to write or draw with your non-dominant hand (I'm right-handed so for Inner Child work I use my left hand). Write to find out what your little child is feeling, or wanting, or just say 'hi' to him or her.

Drawing can help, but you must unhinge yourself from the world of 'perfect' art work, competition and feeling 'I'm no good at drawing'. Just draw, or paint – go for it. No one else ever needs to see it. It's for you, the little frightened child who went into hiding long ago because it was all so scary.

You must give the process time, but I found the whole thing remarkably illuminating. My hurt Inner Child was bursting to get out, to be heard, to be cared for.

Our inner life consists of our feelings, thoughts, needs and wants, as well as our values, our hopes and our dreams – what is important and meaningful to us… They are vital aspects of who we are… our True Self. No one can take that from us.

JOHN AMODEO

Dialogue

One of the things Lucia suggests in her book is to try to talk to your Inner Child by writing first with your dominant hand, then replying with your non-dominant hand. This went well for me so I strongly recommend giving it a try.

I found that my dominant hand revealed a hugely critical voice – what in Transactional Analysis is called my Critical Parent. (Transactional Analysis is described in detail in the books by Eric Berne and Thomas Harris listed in the resources section. TA is about our OK-ness (the healthy position is 'I'm OK, you're OK') and it offers a powerful way of understanding ourselves and our relationship with others.) So it wasn't just my mother who was putting me down – I put myself down.

I was surprised at this because I had worked so hard at stopping myself from doing 'negative thinking and self-talk' through cognitive behavioural therapy, which included working hard at my own self-help, reading books and going on adult education courses about self-esteem and assertiveness. I really thought I had that sussed, but I was appalled as I saw such deep feelings of self-hatred and nagging criticism filling my pages.

No wonder my little Inner Child ran and hid!

I experimented with having different creatures with me when I became stuck or if feelings became powerful. For example, Killer Whale helped me acknowledge my anger, and although I felt some terror at that, my cuddly killer helped me to begin to accept that bit of myself.

Drawing

It was drawing left-handed that really began to unlock a great deal for me at the start – which again was surprising considering my preference for words, but I was beginning to learn that I needed images too and I was able to connect with the part of me that loved diagrams and mathematical patterns.

Whenever I felt the session wasn't going well I found it really helpful to draw myself as a child. This seemed to unlock the feelings.

Linked with my experiences of holding little Suzie-doll, I was finding a surge of love for the little child inside me. She had to work hard though to get me to listen to her feelings.

Over and over again she would say:

'You aren't listening to me!'

'I'm trying to,' I'd write with my right hand.

'No you're not. You won't listen to my FEELINGS.'

Because it was so painful and frightening to write about the feelings, the drawing eased the way for me to connect more with my inner world.

Drawing gets people out of their rational, analytical, adult frame of mind and immerses them in the Child state. We know that drawing comes predominantly from the right hemisphere of the brain. This is the side that seems to specialize in visual/special perception, as well as emotional and intuitive expression.
LUCIA CAPACCHIONE

Activating our right hemisphere

What Inner Child work does is get us back in touch with the bits of ourselves that shut down through abuse/trauma, or just through ordinary schooling and the influence of adults who wanted us to be like mini adults, not like children.

As children we grow up increasingly using the left side of our brain. Obviously at school we need to learn to be logical, to remember facts and to use verbal reasoning. However, this increasing use of our left brain can unhelpfully get in the way of appropriate right brain thinking.

The bit of us that wants to play and be silly (the creative right side of our brain) is told to grow up. The bits of us that are filled with fear (perhaps when we can't quite grasp what adults want us to do) retreats deep down inside us – out of reach to everyone, including ourselves.

Traumatic feelings are trapped in our right brain, and to heal from abuse and find our True Self, we need to 'touch' that hurt child's feelings and memories – to listen to him or her. And the way to do that is to do creative right brain things such as drawing and anything else that you think of as having fun.

We must keep playing. Older kids need to play, teenagers and adults need to play!

It is as babies that we first feel and learn what to do with our feelings, when we start to organize our experience in a way that will affect our later behaviour and thinking capacities.
SUE GERHARDT

What kind of parent are we?

Lucia says that we tend to parent our Inner Child in the ways that we were parented – in other words, I wasn't looking after my Inner Child very well. That came through clearly as I wrote and drew.

But it's important to note that, in a world where we are a *real* parent to our actual children, we can be the very best parents ever. We can make a conscious decision to be good parents and break the chains of poor parenting that have been passed down the generations.

It is not true that if we were abused as a child we will be abusive parents (although sadly some survivors do go on to abuse their own children). We will all make mistakes of course, but if we give our little ones love, freedom to be who they are, lots of play and nurturing activities (such as cuddles and creative activities like looking for bugs or painting), and do silly things with them like singing funny songs in the bath, then our kids – and their children – stand the best chance of being joyful people at peace with themselves.

If you feel that you are being a bad parent to your children, seek help.

What Lucia is getting at is that it is our adult self that isn't looking after that Inner Child bit of us that needs love and nurturing.

Ruth Rabbit

As I tried to stop myself being such a Critical Parent to my Inner Child, I was becoming aware of the positive relationship that I now had with Ruth. She was in some sense 'parenting' me in a new and different way. She was:

• accepting of me even when I was in a rage or refusing to say anything

• comforting when I cried, especially when those tears showed my incredulity that anyone could hurt a tiny child

• nurturing my growing sense that I had no need to feel guilt and shame.

I was experiencing from her the kind of parenting that I needed to give my Inner Child. So when I saw Ruth Rabbit in a charity shop, she came to stay. Ruth Rabbit is rather like Rabbit in the *Winnie the Pooh* books, who runs around making sure that everyone is OK, and with the little rabbit in my pocket I could endure going to work and underground train journeys.

I could now see that the Inner Child work was important – and I had to focus on giving myself more nurturing messages than the Critical Parent outpourings of condemnation that seemed to come from deep within me.

Our inner world

As I worked at holding Suzie-doll and talking to her, and as I wrote and drew left-handed, I was always surprised at what came onto the paper in front of me.

I began to see that the violence in my home as a child was abuse. However hard I tried to say, 'It was nothing', it was abusive.

I could see that my mother was abusive and manipulative, and she was still invading my life and putting me down.

I began to accept that my uncle had sexually abused me, and I could feel sorry for the confused fourteen-year-old as well as the confused girl who couldn't cope with her older brother, who was apparently obsessed with trying to get into her knickers.

As I read more about Inner Child work, it was easier to understand Eric Berne's work on Transactional Analysis, where he shows us the different aspects of ourselves:

- parent self (who sets out rules and regulations – 'don't do that, you ought to do this, you shouldn't do that')

- child self (who feels and reacts in a 'real' way)

- adult self (who thinks, makes decisions, and solves problems).

Becoming the little child

The more I wrote with my left hand the more I began to see the power in this method of healing. I became that little hurt child. I went back to the time of the 'rape' in the park, the stranger, and my mother's attempt at mothering afterwards. I felt the humiliation, the shame, the horror, the confusion. I touched the rage I had felt when my mother had taken the six pennies from me, and the shame and the guilt that came when I looked at her face and knew I had done something terribly wrong.

I didn't get my bar of chocolate. Is that part of the reason why chocolate is my ultimate comfort food to turn to when the world goes horribly wrong?

The more I drew, left- and right-handed, the more I understood and grew close to a terrified child – the me inside me who finds the world so frightening.

If you are finding it hard to do the Inner Child writing and drawing (maybe you've forgotten what it was like to be a child), Lucia suggests that we watch small children, playing or in the shops with parents.

Our Inner Child needs care

There are several signs that our Inner Child needs care:

• when we find ourselves irritable or annoyed but we are not sure why

• when we have physical illnesses that are difficult to diagnose

• when we suffer from depression, stress, burnout or other mental distress.

All these can be signs that we need to listen to our Inner Child.

Crucially we must remember that we are the only ones who can do the re-parenting. Not even a loving partner or therapist can do it for us.

Although [one woman] had some difficulty feeling connected with her Inner Child, she had begun the process of letting the Child speak. That is all it takes to start re-parenting yourself. Remember, it is an ongoing adventure of personal renewal.
LUCIA CAPACCHIONE

Craving love

One of the things I began to understand was the way in which the little child inside us craves love, but instead of listening to those inner needs, we eat too much, or smoke, or take drugs, or drink, or binge on chocolate, or find some other way to try to block out the feelings that our Inner Child is trying to tell us about.

The more I worked on trying to understand my deep feelings, the more I needed fatter crayons and felt-tip pens if I was to let my Inner Child express herself. She had big things to say that needed more scribble, more rage, more space to shout and dance.

You can tempt your Inner Child to creep out because it is play time – time to be who you are.

It's time to listen. Time to let your Inner Child talk:

Suzie (left hand:) Why won't you listen to me?
Adult Sue (right hand): I do try.
Suzie (left hand): No. You don't listen to me enough.
Adult Sue (right hand): What do you want to tell me?
Suzie (left hand): Feel afraid. I'm so sad. Want to find my real daddy. Want him to come and rescue me.
Adult Sue (right hand): Let me hug you.

Freeing the Inner Child

I let my Inner Child spell how she wanted to. Having grown up with taunts like 'You can't spell', no way was I going to let little Suzie feel she 'ought to do this' or 'should do that'. She could do it any way she wanted – and deliberately doing crazy spelling was delicious!

So try to dump the 'shoulds' and 'oughts' and go for creative expression that suits you, such as loud music or doing creative things you were not allowed to do as a child.

Looking back on those months when I worked at Lucia's book I can see that I learned a great deal. But for reasons I'm not sure about, I stopped doing Inner Child work. (My Critical Parent leaps in at this point and says, 'Typical you, can't stick at anything, can you?') But like Transactional Analysis, it stayed with me as a framework for understanding myself better and trying to break some of my chains.

One possible reason I stopped doing it was that it was showing me so much that it was overwhelming. So do try to share what you are doing with someone else – joining a self-help group would be ideal.

KEY POINTS

■ Even years after we start to break our chains there can be a great deal more to 'uncover' and 'recover'.

■ Inner Child work can help us reconnect with the right side of our brain where our little child hurt feelings are trapped and unheard.

■ We can be bad at listening to our Inner Child so we need to learn to re-parent – to love and listen to our inner True Self.

CHAIN BREAKING

1. Look back in this chapter for ways to access your Inner Child. You might want to make a special place where you can write or draw – maybe on big bits of paper.

2. Keep journalling – this might become your usual way of accessing your Inner Child.

3. Set up a place where you can paint, or do clay modelling, or build a doll's house, or knit toys, or make lace, or build book shelves, or make models out of matchsticks, or make greetings cards, or draw spirals or other mathematical patterns – or do something else with your hands that makes you feel good.

You are setting out on your journey to find your True Self.

4. Do you need a 'Ruth Rabbit' to help to touch the recovering part of you? The bit of you that is learning to parent your Inner Child?

5. Try to sit quietly and remind yourself of chains you have already broken, for example, 'I know it's not my fault.'

6. Which of your chains are you going to hack away at today?

7. Giving yourself treats is important – plan some for this week.

Remember

Don't get discouraged with Inner Child work. You need to give it time. When you discover your Inner Child you will find it releases your creativity so you can love and embrace the hurt little child within. This changes your life!

Unaccepting parents – 'Aren't you ashamed of yourself!' – convince us that we will never meet their approval.
PHILIP YANCEY

Able Just To Bear It

Part 3

Understanding the chains

• •

This section is about understanding our fears and learning the reasons why we hurt ourselves. It also suggests some strategies for changing the way we think and breaking the chains of self-harm.

As we struggle to break our chains we can often find that we need more information, or we get stuck and think that we aren't making any progress. This seems to happen to all survivors, so we mustn't give up. We must remember that we have decided to break our chains, and that is what we will do. But getting rid of the guilt, shame, negative thinking, anxiety and confusion will take time.

We're not 'wallowing in it'.
We just need more help and more time.

We've got nothing but time, and it is on our side. This is why we continue to be provided with opportunity to repeat and re-create our lives.

IYANALA VANZANT

10 What's keeping me chained up?

If we can understand more about the problems survivors face through the effects of trauma, we are in a better position to be able to break the chains that pin us down and get in the way of us having a contented life of love and peace.

Not all survivors have all of the problems. For example, lots of survivors don't cut themselves, and I've met survivors who seem to have a realistic sense of their self-esteem – at least they do now they have worked on their healing.

Why we couldn't say 'no'

One of the most obvious characteristics of most survivors who were sexually abused is that we see ourselves as guilty. 'It's all my fault,' we say.

This is one of the most significantly damaging aspects of survivor thinking – and we all seem to do it!

You may have seen the film *Something about Amelia*, in which a young teenager is made to have sex with her father. When Amelia plucks up the courage to disclose the abuse, her mother shouts in rage, wanting to know why Amelia didn't stop it. The thirteen-year-old child is confused and says she doesn't know.

We don't know why we couldn't say 'no'.

But the therapist in the film tries to explain to the mother that Amelia was worried that her father might not love her if she didn't do what he said.

There must be *so many different reasons* why a child can't say 'no'.

It wasn't our fault.

Adult rape victims are sometimes perplexed about why they were not able to prevent the attack. They blame themselves, as if they were the guilty party. (I heard recently that excessive drinking of alcohol is a common feature among some adult rape victims. It's important to note that, to keep ourselves safe, we do need to look after our body and stay alert – something we cannot do if we are drunk. It doesn't make it the victim's 'fault' if they are raped – of course not – but they do significantly lose control and the ability to choose and to say 'no'.)

Shame and low self-esteem

This pair of feelings runs through this book – they are powerful, debilitating, and they keep survivors in their silence.

We dare not tell.

So when a court case of sexual abuse comes onto the television news and someone near us says, 'It obviously didn't happen, because why didn't they say something at the time?' we might want to say that few victims say anything at the time – particularly children, because they often don't know the words to say or how to tell.

Shame, guilt and self-blame are insidious – and so difficult to shift from our inner world where those 'old tapes' are playing the messages we picked up: 'You are hopeless,' 'It was all your fault,' 'You're only good for sex.' This is negative thinking and we need to take positive action to understand it.

I knew [the abuse] was all my fault because we used to play rough and tumble on the carpet sometimes at night and I didn't wear knickers under my nightie so I know it was all my looking as if I wanted it. So I feel the most terrible guilt.

A WOMAN ON A BRITISH TELEVISION DISCUSSION PROGRAMME

It was my fault

An abused child can only assume that it is his fault that his mum has abused him. He is the bad one because it is unthinkable that mum would be bad because she looks after him.

And the seeds of low self-esteem are there within us, ready to be compounded by insensitive teachers, priests, doctors, social workers and often our friends and family too.

Physical abuse – beatings and other appalling things that are done to children – is absolutely horrific, but we need to remember that the emotional abuse that goes alongside any kind of abuse also gives the worst start in life any child can have. And emotional abuse is hidden. So little is done about it.

'I'm no good,' the little five-year-old would say to me, his teacher, as I sat beside him helping him to read.

That view of ourselves as 'hopeless' is one of the earliest chains that we get trapped by and is a very hard one to shift.

Did I enjoy it?

I remember that when working with John I began to be desperately worried that if anything sexual happened with my step-father, I might have enjoyed it. Somehow that made everything very much worse.

I thought John would think me wicked.

I believed myself to be wicked.

When I told John of the sexual incidents in my childhood that I could remember clearly, there were just so many of them. So it had to be my fault, didn't it? Because there were so many different men. I must have been flirting. Leading them on.

For men to expose themselves to you once might be normal. Twice maybe if you were unlucky. But by my count it was about twenty or thirty incidents – sometimes the same man five or six times, some of them relatives, some of them strangers.

I hated myself.

I wanted to be dead.

My eating spiralled out of control.

I felt an overwhelming sense of all-encompassing shame. I believed not just that I was wicked, but that I was evil – something I knew I had felt since childhood – and this was keeping me depressed and anxious.

Loss of trust

If we are abused by a caregiver as a child, one drastic result is that it plays havoc with our ability to trust.

Learning to trust is a fundamental part of life. The little babe in arms has to trust the parents or caregiver for absolutely everything.

Without someone to trust we're not only chained up, but bolted to the floor as well. Without having learned to trust and with our earlier trust shattered:

• How can we make relationships at school when we are thrust through the door and somehow have to survive?

• Do we dare to trust brothers, sisters, parents and cousins?

• How are we going to be able to trust someone enough to love them?

• If we love Mum but she abuses us, can we ever feel safe – anywhere?

I get a shiver down my back in spy films when the characters get to the bit where they say, 'Whom can we trust?' The characters show horror on their faces. There is no firm ground to stand on and all the assumptions being made might be wrong.

Trust is a hugely powerful thing that influences just about every aspect of life.

Dysfunctional family relationships

I loved that word 'dysfunctional' from the very first moment I heard it. I got this mental image of my mother and step-father, dizzy from spinning around too much as they threw plates, bashed through windows and hurled abuse at each other. In reality they sometimes ended up taking it out on us kids (three of us, me in the middle of two boys, all three of us with different fathers).

One of the things I learned with John was that it must have been confusing to live in a family where you never knew what was going to happen next. I was trying to convince John that life as a kid wasn't all that bad for me. Some of the bits were good – my step-father could even be funny, and so could my mother. But you never knew when the volcano would erupt and venom and blood would flow.

'It's not as if it was bad all the time,' I said.

'But it must have been harder not knowing what the rules were or what might happen next?'

I sat and stared at John. I hated it when he upset the firmly held beliefs that I kept as a shield to protect my inner world from seeing what was real.

But I knew he was right. I'd be a hopeless teacher and mother if I kept changing the rules. The kids would never know where they were – they'd be insecure.

I had to admit to myself that it had been utterly awful. In my family of origin:

• no one ever said sorry

• inexplicably life would change from all-out nuclear war to an egg-shell-thin peace. You never knew if you were in for a beating or not – these were random. The only one of us who wasn't hit was my younger half brother (the child of my mother and step-father). He was never wrong – apparently

• there were rules, but they changed without reason, except for two: you must at all times keep Mum happy; and never ever talk back to or in any way annoy The Ernie Monster (my step-father)

• I found the only way to survive was to creep around keeping as low a profile as possible, and retreat to my own room where I could go into my own world that none of my weird family could get into. In that world I was safe and it became reality for me; the other world where I had to sit at the family meal table and so on was the unreal place.

Abusive families raise confused kids – and I think confused kids make easy victims for abusers who prowl around looking for prey. Survivors are so much looking for love, looking for someone to care, so glad of any attention at all; and often we are loners, too scared to be otherwise. That can mean that we get into abusive situations more easily. For example, I spent much of my time alone – I was easy prey.

But I learned young that everything was *my fault. I was to blame.*

'[In families where abuse occurs, abusive acts] happen so frequently that they become not only expected but the child believes that they are brought on by herself.' Children in this situation begin to blame themselves for being abused or mistreated.
MARILYN STRONG QUOTING SCOTT LINES

Frozen out
Another issue that arises for survivors is that they can be frozen out of their family or community. 'Take it all back, then you can come back.'

But we don't want to take it back. We stand by our accusations. We want to do that to feel like a real person at all. (But I completely understand when survivors do back down so they can go back to being part of the family.)

So survivors can have strong feelings of loneliness and isolation.

The loss and grief that we suffered with the abuse, and the loss of safety, trust and so on, is now compounded by the loss of our family around us. We grieve in our loneliness and again seek out help. But help is hard to find, so we resort to our own means of coping, maybe by self-harming or abusing our body in some other way, such as an eating disorder.

I don't think it works to try to heal alone. It works so much better if you can talk to someone about it.
MARTIN AGED 23

Some specific difficulties

Abused people have similar feelings about whoever abused them and whatever kind of abuse they were subjected to, but there are some specific difficulties if the abuser was a teacher, priest, youth leader, father, mother or other primary caregiver.

How would a young child, already abused, even start to cope if he were placed in care or in a foster home, only to be abused there as well?

How would you cope if you were sent away to boarding school and were abused by a teacher? What might that do to your learning? Your sense of trust and safety? How would you deal with the threats not to tell? Or the promise that you are special?

What if someone tells you about the love of God but then abuses you? What would that do to your faith?

Male survivors

The majority of people who are abused are women and the majority of abusers are men, but this can disguise the problems that male survivors have. Their hurt is huge, but they seem to be even more ignored than women survivors.

My mother was abusive, but never sexually. A mother is meant to nurture you, to comfort you when you fall, when you fail, when you are afraid of the dark, and when you need some unconditional love. What a warped view of life could emerge from the pain of having a sexually abusive mother. Where would you go for comfort?

A friend of mine was horribly sexually abused by his much older brother. He spent his teenage years not only with the teenage angst that we all get, but also with worries about whether he was gay or not. He didn't want to be gay (the bullying about it had already started at school), but his fourteen-year-old mind wondered if the abuse meant he already was gay.

He felt there was no one to ask. No one to share with. Eventually he tried to ask his uncle but it was a disaster, so he vowed he would never say anything to anyone ever again.

He longs for love. For a partner. For children.

Being in a self-help group he managed to share at last – despite most of the group being women.

Male survivors of sexual abuse need special attention, whether it was abuse in their childhood, or being seduced by a woman later in life – perhaps getting into something that spiralled out of control, that they didn't really want. It is all too easy to think that a man could never get trapped in that way, but they do – of course. It might not sound very macho, but that in itself can be a huge part of the problem abused men face.

> *Our feelings are the source of our energy; they provide the horsepower that makes it possible for us to accomplish the task of living.*
> M. SCOTT PECK

Strategies for dealing with shame and low self-esteem

1. Accept that the shame we feel is usually not appropriate – nor is the guilt that comes with it.

2. With low self-esteem we usually don't value ourselves enough. But we can change that by doing little things to look after our body – eating well and looking after our nails, for example. Doing these things is much easier than changing our thinking, but I believe that they can help us to change what we think of ourselves.

3. Nurture your Inner Child: listen to him or her; have treats; do things you want to do for a few minutes each day.

> *The surest cure for the feeling of being an unacceptable person is the discovery that we are accepted by the grace of One whose acceptance of us matters most.*
> LEWIS SMEDES

KEY POINTS

- In most abuse it is hard for victims to say 'no'.
- Shame and low self-esteem are common in survivors.
- Difficulty with trusting others is hugely influential in life.

CHAIN BREAKING

1. We need to monitor our negative thinking (see the end of chapter five). Imagine the negative thinking is coming from Eeyore:
'I don't deserve help because I'm bad.' 'I'm hopeless...' 'I shouldn't...' 'I can't...'

What we need to do is identify these negative things that we say to ourselves, then change them with more positive Tigger thoughts.

Tigger challenges the negative with words such as 'I will...' 'I want to...' 'I can...'

You will almost certainly need to write some of this down – just quick jottings will do – for example, noticing how much you put yourself down. You are not likely to remember how much you do it and be able to change it unless you make a commitment to monitor your thinking over a couple of days. Get people to help you if you can.

2. Write/draw/paint 'I feel shame about...'

Remember
We can't change what happened in the past but we can change our feelings about it – and this will transform our life.

Nothing which has entered into our experience is ever lost.
WILLIAM ELLERY CHANNING

11 Fears and phobias

The more I tried to be OK and to manage my flashbacks and nightmares, the worse my phobias became, particularly my fear of having people behind me, and of hearing people eat, or being near people eating, or hearing any kind of mouth noise (swallowing, people kissing noisily on the television, and people smacking their lips as they talked).

Then I had a bad cold and over the space of a week I developed a panic about my own swallowing that I still have, though it is much better. The terror comes from feeling catarrh in my throat and needing to swallow it, followed by intense fear that I will never be able to swallow again, and what I think is something close to a spasm in my throat that seems to prevent me from swallowing. Lying down in bed is the worst (and being at the dentist). It feels as if I need to swallow and I have to sit up to do that, but it can take anything from a few seconds to a couple of minutes to be able actually to swallow.

Sometimes I used to get so panic stricken I would have to get out of bed, crying and out of control.

I suppose to some readers that sounds a bit stupid – pathetic even. But to me for something like fifteen years I've dreaded getting a cold. One winter just a couple of years ago I got bronchitis and was ill for about three weeks, and it was the swallowing panics that changed this from being an ordinary winter illness into something close to repeated terror.

Behaviourist therapy

I was offered help from a behavioural psychiatrist who said he would give me some treatment which involved me sitting through noisy eating. He said this would make me better. I discovered that this kind of treatment works really well – which surprised me. But I cared much more about what was behind these phobias. Why were they trapping me into such an unpleasant life? Even if I could end up feeling that eating was not going to annihilate me, what about the fear of being near men, the agonies on public transport, the nightmares, the flashbacks that crashed into my life, ruining my day?

Added to that, the clinic where I needed to go for the treatment was so noisy and crowded that I couldn't cope with the waiting room. It meant a regular time each week, which my work at the time just wouldn't allow. I had to go on working. Being a workaholic was my survival mechanism in order to be able to cope with life.

Yes, I wanted to be able to sit with my family and eat a meal. But I thought it *better to understand why I had the phobia in the first place.*

How do phobias arise?

I've read several things about phobias and Obsessive Compulsive Disorder but there seem to be many theories about why these odd things happen. Therapy can help to get rid of them, and I know people who have been hugely helped even by short spells of intensive therapy.

It seems that some difficult event happens, and something inside us gets 'stuck'. Surprisingly, getting rid of these 'stuck' memories (that show themselves in obsessions and phobias) is apparently easier than we might think – easier than some aspects of chain breaking anyway.

Fears and phobias can hit anyone, not just people who have been abused, so if you are struggling with these issues, your doctor might be able to help you find specialist help.

What we can do is to try to work out what the fears are about through writing or some kind of visual creative activity, and of course through our Inner Child work.

As I sat and talked to little Suzie-doll I worked out that one aspect of my fear of being near or hearing people eating related to my stepfather. I sat to the right of him at the meal table as a child and his jaw would click – he was quite a noisy eater. I was very close to his right hand and never knew when he was going to rage at me or hit me. Sometimes bits of his spit escaped onto me or my food.

Three new Eeyores

As the weeks went by talking with Ruth, I found that I was having to talk about things I didn't want to think about.

I was in that phase when therapy was getting much worse, without any promise at all that things might eventually get better.

I took Eeyore with me every week to therapy, and Ruth seemed completely unphased when I turned up with three brand new furry Eeyores as well. Old Eeyore was now so loved that his tail had fallen off, his mouth had disappeared (which was good because I could tell him anything and he couldn't tell anyone else), and his eyes had rubbed off.

We had tried to buy another grey Eeyore but they were very hard to find. So when we did find grey ones, David insisted I have three of them – 'just in case'.

Struggling with life

I didn't know how I could go on. Life was so very painful. I was lecturing at London University and the stress of that was huge, and as well as that I had my writing, including a major education project that seemed to go on and on, relentlessly.

At one therapy session I was trying to find my way through it all, but I was thoroughly chained up and crying because of the horrible thoughts that kept popping into my mind. Ruth left the room for a bit and returned with a small black bear, called Able Just To Bear It. He was Ruth's bear, but she gave him to me and said I could keep him.

I was utterly amazed. How could someone care about me enough to give me one of their bears? I couldn't get my head around that at all.

But Ruth explained about Able Just. When life is awful, he reminds me that I am Able Just To Bear It. Immediately I fell in love with this utterly cute bear who I discovered could sit at the bottom of my bag, or in my pocket when I was out of the house (a hard place to be), and I could even hold on to him without anyone knowing. He accompanied me when I was lecturing. He sat on my desk beside me as I wrote.

Able Just survival strategies

I learned to touch Able Just and think of the survival strategies for managing life I was learning with Ruth:

- I am Able Just to manage life.

- I need to cling on tight to my creatures.

- OK, life isn't great at the moment, but Ruth says it will get easier.

- When I am frightened on the underground train if a man comes near me, it isn't Ernie. Ernie is dead. He cannot touch me now. (If your abuser is still around, your Able Just strategies must include your safety.)

- I'm not a wicked person.

- My body is remembering some things from when I was very young indeed. This might turn out to be abuse, it might not, but I must listen carefully to what my body is trying to tell me.

- I am Able Just to do this because Ruth is there to help me. She is not going to disappear. (One of my greatest fears.)

Sex and violence

One of the hardest things to talk about with Ruth was my strange sense of feeling deep hatred as a surge in my vagina. She linked this to the role violence can have in sex.

This terrified me.

I didn't want to talk about it. Violence horrifies me. Sex is confusing. Put them both together and I space out to avoid the chaos that comes into my body.

I knew by this stage that some of the confusion I experience with sex – such as an overwhelming nausea and a terror of being unable to breathe – could all be related to things with my step-father.

Violence meant my step-father. I wanted it all to stay dead just like him. But I can see that for some survivors there can be a link between sex and violence, and that might need specialist help to unravel.

I didn't really want my confusions unravelled, so what I did was find Able Just.

I knew I was still full of self-hatred – I couldn't look in mirrors – but Able Just was there with me. I knew I felt 'evil' because of the surge of aggression I felt in my vagina when I hated something desperately. (It's not a 'turned on' feeling.) I've worked at trying to understand this surge of hate, but so far it stays in my mind as confusion, and Able Just helps me to touch the emotion that tells me that I'm OK. I see it now as a part of me, and that is how it is. I'm Able Just To Bear It.

Strategies for dealing with anxiety, fears and phobias

1. If you are offered help to deal with phobias, go for it. The behaviourist stuff I'm assured can really work, even over a short space of time.

2. Look at my list of Able Just survival strategies above. Write some like mine that apply to your circumstances. You could write them on a bit of card and take them with you when you go out, or put them in places where you are likely to see them at times of need.

3. Some kind of mantra can help. Mine was 'It isn't Ernie, I'm safe' said over and over again. Your mantra would be different – see if you can make one up.

4. Phobias are about something, and understanding that something can go a long way to breaking our chains. Commit yourself to getting rid of them. Find out what it is that is 'stuck' somewhere inside you.

KEY POINTS

■ Fears and phobias can profoundly affect our life.

■ Phobias can be helped by therapy.

■ Some fears of sex and the linking of sex and violence might need specialist help.

CHAIN BREAKING

1. Another way to get rid of anxiety is to counteract the negative stuff in your brain with positive things. If you are a ruminator like me, sitting around thinking negative thoughts – such as rage at our abuser/s – is going to make us more anxious, not less. (Although appropriate anger is necessary to provide the motivation and energy to heal, see chapters twenty and twenty-one.)

Try writing a list of good things about yourself to counteract the negative stuff – OK, I know you don't think there are any, but there are. Are you caring? Tenacious? Skilful at managing money? A good listener? Funny? Good at recycling? Do you use cleaning products that don't harm the environment?

2. Some of our fear and anxiety can arise because of the intrusive

thoughts and flashbacks that shoot through our mind unpredictably. Look back to the list of strategies for dealing with flashbacks on page 38 and decide which ones you could use to decrease your anxiety.

3. Talk about your fears and phobias. Write/paint/draw them in stories about your childhood and your later life. It can be through 'story' that we find ourselves – we find who we are. Share your story at your self-help group.

4. How are you doing so far with this book? Do you need to go back to something to give it more thought?

Remember
Trauma can affect the whole of our body. You may feel physical pain or just feel generally unwell.

This will all pass.

> We had discussed the possibility of going to Australia... How could anyone who couldn't even cross the road alone contemplate going to Australia? [To be with her husband David Sheppard playing for England in the cricket test match. But the trip went well.] As the Canberra moved out of Sydney Harbour, I was full of relief that I'd managed... David had played well, so another anxiety – that I'd be blamed ... for a poor performance – was laid to rest.
>
> GRACE SHEPPARD

12 Hurting ourselves

One thing that almost all survivors seem to do is hurt themselves in some way. We do this hurting deliberately even if sometimes we try to make out it was an accident.

These self-destructive actions can be horribly misunderstood, but I suppose that is to be expected since we are often quite unclear ourselves why we do them.

It's not just hurting our physical body, because we do it mentally as well, when we 'beat ourselves up' about something, or tell ourselves we are hopeless.

Understanding why we hurt ourselves is vital.

Body memories

I wonder if there is some link between so many of us abusing our body, and our memories also coming back through our body? I've tried to ask a few people about this but no one seems clear if there is a link.

I believe that what lies behind our self-destructive acts is our hatred of our body, of ourselves, of our lives as they are at the moment. But it is much more complicated than that because sometimes the things we do, although seen by health workers and our carers as negative and destructive, can actually be helping us to heal.

That probably sounds crazy.

But over and over again survivors will tell of the great relief that they feel after they have cut themselves or made themselves sick.

These things we do seem in some weird way to be needed to relieve stress and to help us feel that we can go on.

So when we give ourselves a hard time because we just did something we wish we hadn't (and now hate ourselves), we do need to remember that what we did just might have defused something much more destructive, or relieved us of stress that might have exploded.

I'm not saying we shouldn't try to stop doing those self-destructive things – not at all. I'm saying that for the times when we are working through the pain, our self-destructive actions can be something of a safety valve.

Bingeing and throwing up, or cutting ourselves, probably won't break any chains, but it might get us through today and one step closer to 'uncovering' and 'discovering' our issues.

The things we do

Survivors have a whole range of ways of attacking their body – actions or results that can be seen (such as scars, bump, bruises and so on). These things include:

- cutting – often arms and legs with razor blades

- burning skin with cigarettes etc.

- picking scabs

- picking or biting toe or finger nails to the point of drawing blood

- pulling out hair

- headbanging

- face slapping

- kicking or punching walls and other hard objects so that great pain is felt.

Most of these things are done in secret and are hidden with clothing or bandages. So these things are visible but often hidden from others.

There are other things we do that cannot usually be seen, except when we change the size of our body.

- Starving ourselves and other chaotic eating habits.

- Bingeing and throwing up.

- Taking large quantities of laxatives and so on.

We also do the internal thought self-destructive things, the mental things, the negative thinking that can be so hard to change, such as:

- I can never recover from abuse.

- I deserve to be this unhappy.

- There is no point in trying to get better, nobody will want a relationship with me because I'm unlovable.

- It's all my fault so I must go on punishing myself.

Self-harm and I have an ongoing relationship. I try to 'divorce' it, but it keeps clinging on and won't let me go!
CLAIRE

Suicide attempts

Self-destruct mode is dire, and in desperation some survivors often reach the point of wondering if they can go on with life. I know that for me, if anti-depressants or some other toxic drug were available, it was all just too tempting. I wanted out of life. I just couldn't stand it any longer.

The trouble is, once you have had suicidal thoughts, or have made attempts, it can become a dangerous habit.

We do need to address this honestly and we really need to talk to someone about it.

• Working through the pain and learning to break the chains is so utterly painful that suicidal thoughts are maybe to be expected.

• Depression sets in and it is hard to believe that life will ever get any better.

• We've tried so hard. But it still feels awful.

• We are exhausted:

• People keep saying, 'It was all such a long time ago, move on, forgive and forget,' and all that other kind of destructive advice that gets thrown at us so that we feel even more useless, hopeless and stupid. At least being dead would end all that.

But if we do take all our tablets, or cut much deeper to get an artery, or whatever we are planning, by far the most likely thing we will end up doing is permanently damaging ourselves – maybe becoming a 'vegetable' in a hospital bed for the rest of our life, or cutting a tendon so that although we live, we lose the use of a limb.

It is crucial to remember that committing suicide is a permanent solution to what is almost always a temporary problem.

I know that 'temporary' for some of us means decades, so it is hard to believe it is ever going to get any better.

BUT...

I made quite a few attempts to get out of our weird world (some of them I think were rather half-hearted and were probably more about 'please help me' than 'I want to die'). But some were determined attempts at death, once succeeding (I was dead for several minutes), but the doctors managed in the end to save me – just.

Thinking of that now is so devastating.

I think what I might have done to my children, to my partner, to the rest of my family. What would it have been like for my kids to be saying now to some therapist, 'My mother killed herself when I was eight'? Tears well up in my eyes whenever I think of it. My spine tingles with fear. The horror of what I nearly did haunts me in the small hours.

I thought my children would be better off with a new mother. David needed a better wife.

So I thought.

But I was utterly and totally wrong.

How can I say this loudly enough?

Recently I met a lovely young woman who had small children, and she was saying *exactly* what I used to say: 'If I kill myself the kids will get a better mother.' She was hurting so much she just wanted out of it all, and I saw the old bit of myself in her – the conviction that the world would be a better place if she were dead.

I assume therefore that this is likely to be a reasonably common phenomenon.

I didn't know how to say loudly enough to the honest woman sitting with me that she was so totally wrong.

Her children would weep for their mother, who had left them alone.

She was the best mother in the world for them.

It is the abuse that makes us think so little of ourselves that we can only make sense of the world if we annihilate ourselves.

Any suicide is devastating for those left behind.

Cutting and suicide

Cutting is often misunderstood as a suicide attempt when usually it isn't – there has been quite a bit of research into that (see *A Bright Red Scream* in the resources section).

Cutting, like other apparently self-destructive acts, is a way of relieving tension. It is a way of feeling well enough to keep going. It is the relief needed to still a racing mind, a way of believing that life could be tolerable if we just could see the blood – feel some real pain that we can also see.

The trouble with cutting is it leaves scars that could be with us for the rest of our lives, and can trap us in prejudice.

Some survivors report being mistrusted at work once their scars are detected. There is the assumption that if we were once cutters, we are likely to abuse the children in our trust. Or if we were cutters, we can't possibly be given promotion in the firm because clearly we are not to be trusted.

It's the same thing as when people discover we have been depressed, or we have been in a mental hospital, or we take tranquillizers, or we do anything that makes that other person think, 'What a weirdo.'

Our vulnerabilities are liable to show up the soft spots in others, who are likely to try very hard not to think about our pain so that they can avoid thinking about their own inner pain. So they may hit out at us instead.

More research needed
Self-harming is the focus of research because doctors don't understand it enough. And it isn't just abused people who self-harm. Other 'big' events can spark it off – for example, it can become a problem in someone suffering from ME (post-viral fatigue syndrome) or if a parent dies.

We know self-harming makes us come back from the totally-numb-can't-feel-anything state that we live in sometimes – *at least we feel something*. That brings us back to the present and helps us to feel 'grounded' in reality.

Let's hope that research sheds more light onto self-harming because it can be a huge problem for survivors – partly because some nurses who patch people up from the cuts and so on don't understand what is going on. Years ago a nurse stitched up my hand with no anaesthetic. He told me he did that to teach me not to be so stupid. I'd slashed my wrist and hand across a window I'd just punched. I was in a mental hospital and had just received a letter from my mother. Believe me, slashing my arm was a reasonable response!

Here are some more facts about self-harm from the Samaritans website (see the resources section for more websites).

- Although self-harm is not the same as attempted suicide, those who self-harm are more likely to go on to take their own lives.

- Girls are more likely to self-harm than boys.

- Adolescents who self-harm are likely to have fewer people they feel they can turn to.

- Young people with more problems – at school, at home or with friends – are more likely to self-harm.

- The main reason young people give for self-harming is to get relief from a terrible state of mind.

- Nearly half the young people who have self-harmed tried to seek help from someone – mainly their friends and family – before they hurt themselves.

- Those who seek help find it hard to ask for 'professional' help, including from teachers, because they are too embarrassed, or feel their problems aren't important enough.

- Young people are more likely to self-harm if their friends or family have self-harmed.

Alcohol and drugs

One way we try to cope with the trauma is to dull the pain through alcohol and drugs. In the short term it works; that's why we do it. But in the long term these are serious self-destruct strategies that will bring barrow-loads of chains with them, so you do need to get help.

Alcohol can make you seriously depressed – quite unlike the buzz of happiness that the first couple of drinks bring. More than a few drinks and you are likely to spiral down into gloom and even suicidal thinking.

If we keep using something to dull the pain, we're not going to be able to break chains. We'll still be sitting in the same misery this time next year.

Eating disorders

So many survivors I know seem to have some kind of eating disorder. Medical and supportive help for extreme cases can be found (see the resources section).

Chaotic eating is our way of expressing the stress and anxiety our body is under. So monitoring the link between your feelings and eating can be helpful.

People do get better at managing their eating disorder. Some people seem to recover completely. But I have to admit that I am beginning to lose hope about mine, and that is not really typical of the way I usually think. I make myself think of the hopeful things – it is an essential part of managing life, I think, to meditate on the hopeful.

But I still binge. It is as if I cannot control it. I can't make myself stop. But when I think about that I can only say, 'You are pathetic.'

I believe the thing to do when we feel as if we will never be able to stop our self-destructive behaviour is to list what we have managed to do so far.

On my list is:

1. I don't often starve myself now. (As I edit this for the last time I realize that I do it more often than I like to think I do.)

2. I've promised myself never to make myself sick again.

3. I do sometimes manage to stop in the middle of a binge and walk away. I'm pleased with myself if I do that.

4. 'See, you can do it.'

Suzie Penguin
Suzie Penguin has to wait for a long time for food in the Antarctic winter, so when food is there, she wants lots of it. Her roly-poly tummy is like

my flabby wobbly bits that get out of control, and when I hug her, I remind myself that there is to be no throwing up and no bingeing.

Recovering from self-destruct mode
It is possible to stop cutting, picking, throwing up and so on. But it is terribly difficult.

I stopped hair pulling in my teens because my mother became aware of it and gave me such a hard time that I had to grit my teeth and stop. I could still do rocking on my bed and headbanging though, because she couldn't see that. I just had to be careful not to let the banging get too loud. I could hit the bit of my

108

head where I pulled out hair so I think that might have been quite comforting, and headbanging was much more painful than hair pulling so that probably helped. I don't have much access to my feelings back then – probably that's a good thing because I was so desperately unhappy I don't really want to get in touch with it any more than I am already.

I think my body coped with my hidden abuse memories by going into depression and I always kept myself busy; three hockey matches a weekend was quite normal for me. When I wasn't busy I had my own world to escape into that no one else had any access to.

I still go into this world – it is essential for my existence. In it I am safe, loved, held, and there are no scary monsters. It is a world of sunshine, puffins, boats, islands, and people I trust. There have been times when this world was 'reality' for me because I had to shut out everything else to survive.

We can stop damaging ourselves, but don't be too hard on yourself – if you are trying to survive emergency stage feelings, cutting, bingeing and so on have short-term value. But remember they are long-term disasters!

Strategies for dealing with eating disorders

1. Admit that you have a problem.

2. Monitor what you are thinking and feeling in your journal and link that with your chaotic eating. I've worked out that under even mild stress I will start to eat. If I don't eat enough at a meal I can end up bingeing.

3. One of my doctors said to me that if I really intended to stop chaotic eating, it was a bit like giving up smoking: 'If you really mean to do it, Sue, one day you will.' That has helped me enormously.

4. I used to accept that I had 'Bad Days'. But now I think that it is better to think in terms of Bad Moments, because at any time a Bad Day can be changed. However much we've eaten, we can stop. There is no need to do the 'Oh, I've wrecked everything. I might just as well eat the rest of the packet' kind of thinking.

5. Try the 'Don't break the law' strategy. I tried this in the last few weeks with my overeating and it worked. This means thinking of your

bingeing/starving as another one of those things we mustn't do. So we mustn't kill someone, or throw a brick through a shop window. Most of us have the power to stop ourselves doing these big things. So how can it be so hard to stop ourselves bingeing or starving or doing whatever we do to harm ourselves?

OK. Hard! But I've found this strategy has really helped me. 'No, I mustn't do that.'

6. I've developed a mantra around eating – 'eat healthily' – and gradually my thinking about food is changing.

Strategies for dealing with self-harming

1. One possible way through is to go 'cold turkey'. Absolutely, immediately stop, and never do it again. You might need help to do this, but it is a really successful strategy. (Get medical help with coming off drugs of any kind. It might be best not to come off supportive drugs such as anti-depressants while you are struggling with breaking your chains.) You could make a gold star chart to record your progress – watch the days and weeks of success and tell yourself you're going to do it! (Yes, you might slip up, but just get going on your plan again.)

2. If you pick and cut, you can divert yourself with safer alternatives. Drawing in red pen on your skin can help. So can pinging an elastic band on your wrist.

If you're into pain, you can put some New Skin (available at pharmacies, intended for covering small cuts) onto a wound. Wow, that hurts! But once it is dry, you can pick at it in a satisfying way.

PVA glue mixed with henna and spread on your skin will dry hard, and when you pick it off there is a brown 'scar'.

Tatoos are great. They hurt like hell and make quite a statement.

3. Do another 'sitting on the end of the bed' time. 'Do I want to be doing this for the rest of my life? No? What can I do about it?'

Make a plan. You can gradually let yourself diminish the things you do if cold turkey doesn't work for you. Write your plan and put it where you can see it. Focus on your successes, not your failures!

4. Try the 'Don't break the law' strategy here as well. You mustn't steal things off the supermarket shelves; you mustn't cut etc.

5. Remember to be kind to yourself. You're a 'goodenough' breaker of the chains of self-harming. So you slipped up seriously. Well, get back onto the plan. Don't do the 'Oh, I've failed today so I might as well give up' thing! Don't give up. You can do it.

6. You are likely to get on better if you have support. Get out there and find a self-help group, or specialist medical help.

Strategies for dealing with suicidal thinking

1. Talk through your suicidal thoughts with someone. (If you have no one to talk to, in the UK you can ring the Samaritans twenty-four hours a day. As well as this, start to gather around you a few supporters who can give you more help.)

It's fairly normal to think about suicide – lots of people do. It might help to show your supporter this book and talk through these strategies.

What we often don't realize is that, although it feels as if no one would miss us and the world would be a better place if we weren't there, this is totally screwed-up thinking! And this kind of thinking will only change if we are talking with supporters. It's a bit like the way you are advised not to make big decisions just after someone you love dies. People can be in such a state of shock that they are likely to make hopeless decisions they will regret later.

That's how it is with suicide: we're in such a state of trauma from the abuse that we will make daft decisions – and if you are dead there is no chance to change your mind.

2. Learn to accept that depression hits survivors, and suicidal thinking is common in depression. Write yourself a note about that and stick it near the kettle. Near your bottle of tablets (or whatever you have decided to use to kill yourself) put a cuddly toy, or a note saying something from this chapter. The bit about the permanent solution to a temporary problem on page 104 would be a good choice.

3. On the worst days, remind yourself that you survived the abuse, and you can survive this.

4. Spend time going through this book looking at the coping strategies. These can help us through the toughest times and remind us that we are valuable human beings who have been horribly damaged – but we can survive.

5. Get out into the fresh air if you can and search for something beautiful: the moss on a tree, the rainbow of colours of oil in a puddle etc.

Try to distract yourself during this walk and plan something positive to do when you get back home, such as making a fruit smoothie, or watching a funny video. You might not feel like watching something funny, but *make yourself do it*. Remind yourself that your life will get back to being OK. What is happening at the moment is a temporary phase.

KEY POINTS

■ Most survivors tend to hurt themselves in some way.

■ We can learn strategies that can change what we do and what we think.

■ Using self-harming as a way of coping may be OK for now, but in the long term we must learn to give it up.

■ Suicide is a permanent solution to a temporary problem – so it isn't really a solution at all and is likely to traumatize those we leave behind.

CHAIN BREAKING

1. Write/draw/paint how your chain breaking is going. What have you achieved? Keep positive. For example, 'I'm not biting my nails so much.'

2. Take an hour out and listen to music or go for a swim or a walk.

3. Make a poster of your progress by cutting up magazines and sticking pictures on a piece of paper to show your feelings.

4. Draw an enormous garbage bin and write or draw in the bin all the things you want to dump.

5. Hurl pebbles into the sea.

Remember
Slashing your arms is definitely better than slashing someone else's arms – but you deserve a better life than that.

Working through this book is likely to be demanding. Be patient. Be kind to yourself. Have treats.

Having come out the other side of an eating disorder I really do believe that we do not need to live hung-up about our bodies and food. People can live lives which are deeper, freer and happier than that.
JO IND

13 False memories?

Because of the ways in which my memories of early sexual abuse came back to me, I was left with considerable fear that I had made it all up.

Surely I would have remembered it?

So I've found this chapter very difficult to write because I am aware of the huge problems that so many survivors have of:

• not being believed

• not believing their own returning memories

• general total confusion with life and everything that seems to descend on people when they try to face the perplexing issue of false memories.

But I want to explore what is going on when we have returning memories, and the problems we get into.

If you are like me and have, or have had, considerable doubts about your memories, or if your abuser vehemently denies what happened, then this might be a hard chapter to read. You might want to read it on a day when you feel strong, or read it with a supporter.

I don't believe you

When a mother doesn't believe her confused eight-year-old daughter as the child tries to tell her that her older brother has raped her, the scene is set for that daughter to struggle with life for years. The trauma of the rape is compounded by the trauma of not being believed.

Some survivors are thrown out of their family until they take back accusations, and the loud denial from the perpetrator soon drowns out the small tortured voice of the victim.

The small boy whose older brother is raping him runs to his parent, but he cannot explain. He tries, but the threats from the older brother terrify him. So the little boy finds other ways to 'explain'. He wets the bed. He cries and hugs his parent, looking for a safe place to be.

But he is told, 'Boys don't cry.' He is told to grow up. Now his parent is just as scary as his older brother.

He invents a dream world where he is safe. Where he is loved.

He is likely to take years to work through his pain as an adult.

He needed to be believed.

What is truth?

One major problem with abuse is that it is so hard to get to the truth of what actually happened. We all know that two people present at the same incident will give slightly different versions – police have real trouble with this after traffic accidents – and in families we know we see things one way, and others view things differently. We can be giving as faithful a report of the incident as we can, and still come up with a different version from someone else.

This is disconcerting.

But it is a crucial thing to remember when we think about abuse. We mustn't always think that our account is the only true and accurate one, but at the same time we must learn to hang on to our version sufficiently to respect ourselves.

This can be really hard, especially when our abusers snarl at us, 'I never did that, you are lying.'

Too trivial to remember

When my uncle (my mother's brother and my only adult male blood relative) put his hands on my breasts as he hugged me when I was a teenager, he might well have had no memory in later life of doing that. Maybe for him it was so trivial and so ordinary that he simply would not retain memory of doing it. In those days grasping the boobs of your only niece might have been acceptable – I even have a photo of him and me, his hand coming under my arm and holding me on my breast.

If I had challenged him about it (he died quite a few years ago and I never referred to what he did), I wonder if he would have denied it?

Probably he would.

There are two different explanations of his possible denial:

- He forgot what he did.

- He remembered but lied.

The fact is that I loved this uncle dearly and had myself put the whole thing out of my mind. I 'forgot'. The memory came back alongside the other returning memories, but what was unusual about this memory of my uncle was that at fourteen of course I could 'remember' it – just as I remembered the 'rape' when I was six. But somehow it had gone into some limbo place in my mind, half in and half out of memory.

Is it true?
The trouble is, we can never know what is inside another person's head. We can never really know their motive for what they say or do. We might think someone is lying, whereas they might not remember, or might have a different memory from ours, or a different interpretation of the incident – because presumably key incidents run and re-run through their memory as well as ours.

I think that as we run memories through our minds (often unaware we are doing that), it is possible for those memories to change. We don't change them in order to mislead anyone, or to lie to others or ourselves. But the memories must get changed as we dream and as we remember something triggered by something else that happens.

We accuse ourselves
Inevitably survivors are confused. It is hard to give an exact chronological account because our emotions are muddled.

We doubt ourselves.

We accuse ourselves of making it all up.

For people like me who were (or think they were) abused as very young children, our memories are of course hazy because they are pre-verbal. Things get muddled up inside dreams, nightmares and flashbacks. But these can be vague, misty, almost unreal, and we doubt ourselves.

Sometimes we doubt the whole of our being.

Gathering evidence
One of the things that Ruth helped me to do was to gather 'evidence' of the abuse. She never ever pushed me into that, but I began to notice how she would say something like, 'What do you think that means, Sue?'

She let me see things for myself, gently guiding me.

It must have been really frustrating for her when I would zoom back into my safe zone of 'No, nothing happened – I made it all up'.

We considered together how my step-father would come into the bedroom during holidays in Scotland when we all slept in the same room. He would watch me get undressed, and however much I tried to cover myself up, he would stand there, grinning, leering, laughing. He would even make comments and I found it all intensely uncomfortable – and wonder now if I wanted my mother to come and protect me. Maybe by then I had given up on her.

Ruth and I talked about his behaviour when I reported to the police a man who kept exposing himself to me when I walked my dog across the fields when I was seventeen. Somehow my step-father even managed to muscle in on talks with the woman police officer. He smiled. He went on smiling. He was enjoying it. I was in embarrassed agony.

Where was my mother?

Ruth and I talked about my step-father's extreme violence – and how he would 'do things' upstairs with my older half-brother (whom my step-father hated). I could hear my brother grunting then crying, but my mother would keep saying, 'Don't you go up there.'

It was a mystery.

Yes, he could have been abusing him – but why would my mother let it go on?

Ruth and I put together a kind of package that was my step-father. A brutal, selfish man who got his own way by using violence and threats, and who tended to leer at me and smile when sexual things were being talked about. He read sexy books, taking them on holiday with brown paper covers on them, threatening my younger brother and I if we dared look at the cover. (Mostly my older brother didn't come with us on holiday.)

He was dishonest in business, openly saying he was cheating the tax man.

Of course, none of that picture of him means he definitely would abuse a step-daughter, but he was hardly Mr Niceguy.

He took what he wanted when he wanted and in the ways he wanted, so my bottle of milk being taken away and a penis put inside my mouth did seem possible. I would only have been around eighteen months old when my mother was pregnant with his child (my younger brother), so maybe for sex he turned to me?

My mother would often tell the story of how I used to rock my cot so wildly that I would 'walk' it across the room and Ernie had to bracket it to the floor.

Why would I need to get out of my cot so violently?

She told how once it was bracketed to the floor I learned to push out the bars sideways and jump on the mattress, causing the cot base to fall out! My mother found these stories funny. So did I until the returning memories.

None of my 'evidence' proves anything. But if you put it all together and consider it as a whole, you have a pregnant mother, a grabbing man and a baby desperate to get out of her cot.

Evidence from photos
To my astonishment I found an early photo of me with The Ernie Monster, me sitting on his lap – I'm about two. I have my finger in his mouth and he has his finger in my mouth.

I felt dead inside.

I showed the photo to Ruth and she said, 'What do you make of that, Sue?'

I just burst into tears. The image of the penis in my mouth was still disturbing my sleep and giving me huge problems with swallowing and coping with a cold.

In the photo I'm wearing my cream silk dress that years later my mother told me she had made from some silk my grandparents brought back from their travels. It has a huge hem on it and I was still wearing the dress when I was four.

It's what I'm wearing in the earliest memory I can recollect – a time when my mother left me on my own when my brother was taken to hospital with scarlet fever. I have no idea how long she left me, but I can almost touch my feelings of terror at being abandoned.

You will never know for sure
Ruth often said to me that I would never really know exactly what happened. I might one day feel 'sure' there was something there, but I could never know with one hundred per cent certainty – and I would have to live with that.

I've learned to live with that, and so have other survivors.

It is a little easier now to say, 'I was sexually abused as a child,' without fearing I'll be struck down by a thunderbolt!

Under stress from a flashback or nightmare I go straight back to 'It never happened, I made it all up, I'm wicked'. These thoughts are accompanied by intense fear of being so wicked God will reject me – despite my firmly held belief that God loves us all unconditionally.

Honourable therapists
Ruth and I would often talk about false memory syndrome and she would say, 'Do you think John pushed you into your memories?' I knew he hadn't.

When I told him about the stranger 'rape' in the park when I was six, he said he'd wondered if there was something like that in my childhood.

'Did John suggest to you that you had been sexually abused?' Ruth asked.

No. He never did that.

'He would never have done anything like that,' I would tell Ruth.

'He was far too honourable, then?' she would say.

'Yes.'

So there it was – any suggestions about sexual abuse had come from me. Never from John.

I could see how a less honourable therapist, or a less well-qualified counsellor, could suggest too strongly, but Ruth would often say, 'But why would any therapist want to do that?'

That's a good question!

Why ever would they? In a mistaken attempt to help their client?

In *A Bright Red Scream*, Marilee Strong says that some therapists might mistakenly think that a client who cuts shows that they have been abused – but that isn't always the case. There are cutters who insist they were not abused. So I'm pretty sure I wasn't pushed into thinking I was sexually abused. If you feel you were that must be really tough.

All of us might just have to make do with, 'You will never really know for certain.'

Hetty Hedgehog

From having had therapy with John I'd already developed the belief that therapy makes things much worse before it gets better. (I suppose what I'm saying here is that the 'uncovery' and 'discovery' phases are just so awful – but essential if we are to get to the 'recovery' stage.)

As I struggled in therapy to make sense of things I realized that I was allowed to be prickly about some things. It's OK to feel really sensitive when family raise something that embarrasses us or hurts us. And we need to allow our family and abuser/s to feel prickly too.

Hetty Hedgehog is only tiny, but she rolls into a ball when she is upset and can give you the most painful prickles if you try to touch her.

Yes, I'm prickly. Upset me and I curl up and go into my own world in order to survive.

And that is OK. We all need to survive.

For supporters of survivors

A problem arises for supporters of survivors, and the problem is particularly stark for carers of children who report abuse.

- You must believe them.

- Act as if you believe them.

- Listen.

- Really listen.

- Believe, believe, believe.

- Yes, the story at first will come out disjointed and jagged, but go on listening – the healing is within, and with, the telling of the story.

Disclosure is difficult enough as it is without a sense that we are not believed.

However, it is probably good for all of us, supporters and 'maybe survivors', to have some level of scepticism. I'd rather err on the side of being a doubter than rush too quickly into believing all my images are about what I think they might be.

KEY POINTS

■ It can be hard to find the truth of our images and memories.

■ We can gather evidence from a variety of sources, such as photos or talking to our family and friends.

■ It's OK to be sensitive and emotional about abuse issues. They are so painful and if we are honest and try to talk about hurts, in the end that will move us into 'recovery'.

■ Find someone who will believe what you say.

CHAIN BREAKING

1. If you doubt your memories, that's fine. There seem to be hundreds of us around and we can take strength from the fact that other survivors sometimes have similar fears such as:

- Did it really happen like that?

- Did I dream that bit in a nightmare?

- What if it isn't true and he can prove it and he comes to beat me up?

- What if it isn't true and he is in heaven and I have to meet him?

- Will God reject me too?

- I'm such a bad person to make up such horrible things.

- It's me who is evil, not him.

- She was my mother – how can I say such terrible things about her?

2. Take one of those statements on that list and write about it in your journal, or make up your own statement of fear.

3. Search through family photos. You might want to put some of them into a scrap book in which you redeem your early life. I started one and as well as things that remind me of childhood I include messages of love (cards and so on) from the loving family I have now. It's good to browse through it on difficult days. (If you don't have a loving family or partner, seek out friends.)

4. Do you need a hedgehog to remind you that it is OK to be prickly?

Remember
You are not alone in this.

To believe with certainty we must begin with doubting.
POLISH PROVERB

Eric

Part 4

Working through the pain

In part four we will discover that there are still many issues for us to work through, such as dealing with feelings of shame, facing the big questions of life and understanding more about the effects of abuse.

We've made the decision to heal, but still we feel chained up. We've done our best to understand a bit more about trauma and the after effects of abuse and we've managed to break some chains, but we still go on hurting.

Then we realize that we need to go on discovering more if we are to find some sense of peace and joy.

We're not wallowing! We're working through the pain.

Love makes everything lovely; hate concentrates itself on the one thing hated.

GEORGE MACDONALD

14 Our feelings matter

While I was working with Ruth I plucked up the courage to go to survivors' meetings. There was usually a speaker, and at my first meeting I totally freaked out when a man ate a biscuit near me.

At the second meeting the speaker was Eric, a lovely teddy bear kind of man who had a soft voice and a smile that helped me to feel less intimidated in this big group.

I knew I kept spacing out, but I bit my lip hard and held onto Eeyore and Able Just, trying to make myself listen carefully.

Eric said something like this:

'Your feelings that you have are *your* feelings. They matter. *They matter enormously because they are your feelings – and you matter*. You must take your feelings seriously – they are trying to teach you something. So listen to them very carefully. They are yours.'

The search for reality

In the eerie world of half-memories and fleeting images that I lived in at that time, this pierced right through all the confusion.

Returning from seeing Ruth earlier that week I was feeling totally freaked out, but I had to go into the shop to get a few basics like bread, milk, fruit and vegetables. At the checkout a man stood too close to me and I began to tremble. He kept making exasperated sounds of wanting me to hurry up. I just had two bags of shopping – easy enough to pick up – but as the assistant gave me back my payment card, I dropped it. I bent down to pick it up, feeling really vulnerable with this man standing so close to me.

I picked up the card, went to put it in my purse but dropped my car keys.

The man said, 'How do fucking women get like that?'

Had I been quick enough I could have turned to him and said, 'You mean you don't know?' or some comment about men – but that would have just been me making a sexist comment back to him.

I just grabbed my keys and fled.

I spent the rest of the day in a high level of panic. Presumably adrenalin was rushing around my body and it was so hard to come out of the 'fight, flee or freeze' state.

I felt angry with the man. Had he not got so very close to me, I might have felt less intimidated. He could even have helped by picking up my card or keys.

But I was delaying him by three seconds and to some people that must be important. None of us knows what is going on in someone else's head and body as they try to get through their day. Perhaps he really was on a life or death mission and needed to speed up.

By the end of that day I managed to feel positive that I'd got through the day, and also that I had felt my anger. In my heavily defended state, too freaked out to do much 'normal' living, at least I'd touched something real – some anger.

Feeling real

At the survivors' meeting on the following Saturday as I listened to Eric, some part of my inner world responded both to the anger I'd felt in the shop and to my thoughts about my real feelings that matter. It was one of those transforming moments and some deep part of myself felt satisfied at sensing real feelings that were *mine*.

In my freaked-out state this was so very important, so on the way home from the meeting I went into the supermarket for some more fresh food and found a tub of 'reduced to clear' teddies that must have been left over from Christmas.

Immediately I adored these teddies. They were incredibly cheap, all wrangle-tangled and just exactly what I needed at that moment. I wanted an 'Eric' to remind me that my feelings are real.

They matter.

They are valid.

They are about some truth within my body.

Eric lives on

Eric became my most loved teddy and I would hold him and remind myself of those feelings that are mine and that matter: so I must take notice of them, respond to them, not block them out.

Reading through this section again years later, my thoughts that day as I listened to Eric the man don't seem all that exciting. But at the time it blew me away and it was one of those transforming moments; and it happened within a large group where I felt very unsafe – something that surprised me, but also pleased me. I think I began to believe in my inner feelings much more and that has stayed with me.

I think trust in our own feelings is one aspect of self-esteem. I know at the time my self-esteem was very low and I think I distrusted any of my feelings. They are such scary things anyway.

Now, to *trust* those inner feelings? That gets close to trusting myself – trusting who I am inside.

Yes. That was what happened that day. I learned to acknowledge my inner feelings. I believe that is what helped me to break the first of my really strong chains.

I think everyone needs an Eric.

KEY POINTS

■ Our inner feelings matter.

■ Learning to trust our inner feelings can help us to feel better about ourselves.

CHAIN BREAKING

1. Write a few sentences about your inner feelings.
   'I feel…'
   'When I think about my inner feelings I…'

2. It's good to talk to our Inner Child to see how he or she is feeling. You might need to do some nurturing because making changes is tough, so you must care for *you*. Nurturing shows us that we love and care for ourselves.

3. Write or draw 'When I've broken a few more chains I'm going to…' (Learn to rock climb? Paint a huge mural called 'How I healed'?)

4. Do you need an Eric?

5. Reflect on how you feel now and the progress you've made. Go back over what you think/write and check it out for negative thinking.

Remember

People who have suffered can become 'wounded healers'. We know how awful life can be for survivors and we can turn our suffering into love and care for other sufferers.

Those who cannot remember the past are condemned to repeat it.
GEORGE SANTAYANA

15 Where is God when it hurts?

The Antarctic has always been a magical place for me because of my childhood wishes to be an explorer (only men did that so I couldn't – all the more reason to want to do it!), and since I was a child I've loved puffins and penguins. So during my years working with Ruth, penguin wildlife documentaries on the television became an important part of our lives.

The mother Emperor penguin lays her one egg, then carefully shifts it onto the father's feet under his fold of feathers to keep it warm. Mum then goes off to feed, leaving dad and the egg to survive in the coldest place on earth. They can only survive because of group cooperation – taking it in turns to be on the outside of the huddle, then gradually edging into the group to get a hug and some warmth.

If anyone gets left out, that means death – for dad and for the egg.

When the chick hatches it must survive in dad's feathery pouch with only a small meal from dad's stomach. To survive, they need mum to come back from her feeding trip.

They wait and wait. If she doesn't come soon, they will die; or dad might decide to dump baby and go back to the sea in order to survive himself.

Mum knows she must get back to her little one, so she leaps onto the ice and waddles and slides up to a hundred kilometres (about sixty miles). That's difficult when you have little legs and funny sticking-out wings that are only useful for swimming.

But mum keeps going; her motherly love and determination to keep her baby alive spur her on.

Motherly love

As I sat and watched the mother penguin, exhausted, calling for her mate, I began to cry. She greets her mate with bill kissing and feeds her little one to give it life.

If only we'd had a mummy like that. A mummy prepared to walk a hundred kilometres. And a daddy who went through the harshest environment on the planet in order to keep us safe and warm.

But lots of us didn't have parents like that, and like the little orphan penguins, we were left to struggle on as best we could.

The Antarctic snow was red with the blood of those babies that didn't make it and were gobbled up by marauding bands of skuas.

Some of us don't make it. The NSPCC in Britain reports that one child a week is killed by a parent.

One child a week!

Mummy Penguin

I found a Mummy Penguin in a toy shop, complete with Baby sitting on her feet, and it was a time for me to admit to Ruth that my mother had been abusive. She used to hit me a lot, sometimes across my face, and I remember banging into the wall when she hit me hard.

I took a long time to realize that my mother's abandonment was abusive, as was her manipulative behaviour and the way she constantly put me down ('You'll never come to anything').

So Mummy and Baby Penguin sat on my desk beside me as I thought my way into healing those memories of a mother who wasn't very caring.

Holding the tiny defenceless chick, I could touch that bit of me that was so hurt. I was beginning to see the healing power that my creatures have.

• They make the pain explicit.

• They make me acknowledge that some inner bit of me was, and sometimes still is, hurt.

• They provide a way for me to incorporate that hurt into my inner world in a way that is less painful. I've looked at it – and by doing that I've robbed the pain of some of its power to go on hurting me.

Where was God?

I knew I was healing as my family of creatures grew, but there was one question that came up again and again:

Where was God when I was being abused?

'If he loves me, why didn't he stop it?' is the thought that goes through our minds. Over the years, colleagues at work and so on have asked me how I can possibly manage to believe in a God of love despite earthquakes, tsunami, and children starving or dying of cancer.

We can put the wicked deeds done by murderers and so on down to human evil and greed – people putting themselves first, and people being so damaged in their early life with no safe and secure place to be that they become mentally imbalanced. But earthquakes, floods and tsunami are harder to make sense of, and to be honest I don't have an answer to where such pain comes from.

I have read books about this problem (if God is so powerful and loving surely he could stop earthquakes happening?) and no one else seems to have a really good answer either – including theologians. So I think that my view is as valid as anyone else's and this is that:

GOD WEEPS AS WE WEEP.

> *Of course, it's easy enough to say that God seems absent at our greatest need because He is absent – non-existent. But then why does He seem so present when, to put it quite frankly, we don't ask for Him?*
> C.S. LEWIS

I believe this Great Creator wanted us to have freedom to choose, so we can believe in the existence of a loving God or not. It is up to us.

I also think this Great Creator, having made a beautiful world, left it free to run according to its own rules: so the outer crust of the earth is still cooling down, causing the earthquakes. The weather is also free to just keep on going, fluctuating as the wind and ocean currents move in their unpredictable ways. So we get floods – greatly helped by human stupidity in places where too many trees have been cut down, or houses have been built on flood plains etc.

We have freedom.

The universe too has 'freedom' to run according to what we have come to call the laws of science, such as gravity. (If you drop a paper weight off your desk and onto your foot, it hurts.)

Sheltering under a wing

My image of a Loving Creator became Mummy Penguin, who would walk a hundred kilometres to get to me. She would let me run into her pouch of feathers when I felt insecure.

I've never been good at the whole idea of God as father – no thanks,

I already have a step-father, a father whose name I had, and a real biological father who left me when I was three weeks old. That's more fathers than anyone needs. So I go with the idea of a mother God who will shelter me at times of need. (As a child I loved my mother.)

This God also collects all my tears in a bottle, an image from the Bible in the Old Testament which I love.

Our tears are valued and understood and this gives me hope.

> *[God] transforms pain, using it to teach and strengthen us, if we allow it to turn us towards him.*
> PHILIP YANCEY

Holding safe

Ruth said that she could 'hold' all the 'junk' I talked about when I saw her. I could leave it in her room, then walk free of it out into the world. I wanted to leave Baby Penguin with her – Ruth was in some way looking after the baby bit of me that wanted to be held – and in some ways that helped me to see that the mental distress I was in was containable. I could leave it behind and walk free – well, reasonably free. Enough to exist for the next few days before I saw her again.

I was learning to 'hold' my own pain a bit by making myself do relaxation exercises and deep breathing. I joined a gym to run off my excess weight because I was comfort eating and bingeing.

I still could only feel completely safe in my safe space in my bedroom.

Little Lamb

David bought me Little Lamb during a time when I was freaked out on most days. I instantly loved her because of her obvious need for love and protection. I was recognizing my need to be 'shepherded' – to be held and loved.

Little Lamb so clearly needed to be cared for and this helped me not to keep insisting that I was 'fine' and that 'nothing happened'. Through holding her I would let myself admit I needed to accept any offers of love and protection that were going, including learning to love and value myself more.

I can't understand why a Loving God would let any of us go through abuse any more than I can know why little children get leukaemia. What I do understand though is that it is OK to be in a rage that we were left to suffer the abuse, and it is OK to be puzzled.

Despite it all I believe I am loved and 'held', and that gives me the hope and energy to go on living.

KEY POINTS

■ Children suffer when adults don't care enough or protect their children.

■ It's OK to scream at God, 'Where were you?'

■ It's difficult to understand why any God of love would let so much human pain happen.

■ Love, care and protection are there for us if we seek them out.

■ I believe God weeps when we weep.

CHAIN BREAKING

1. Find a creature or a picture that represents love, care and holding for you and put it on the wall or on a special shelf where you keep your treasures for healing.

2. How are you doing with your strategies for dealing with anxiety (see the end of chapter eleven)? Are you better at relaxation? Taking time out to de-stress can add a great deal to the quality of our lives. Swimming or dancing or gardening can all de-stress us – if we enjoy them. Walking down the garden with a cup of herbal tea can give us a moment in the day to connect with the Great Creator – to smile at the robin in the tree singing so energetically.

3. Did you make a 'redeeming your childhood' scrap book or box? That might help you to claw back some of what you feel you have lost. It can be a focus for our grieving (we must grieve about our lost childhood) and a way to celebrate that we are working at becoming the person we are meant to be.

4. Do you feel angry with God? That's *good!* You are being honest.

Remember

Grief, sadness and anger will gradually get less overwhelming and the whole process is helped when we listen to our Inner Child and become ruthless with our negative thinking. As we break chains we will begin to feel more powerful; we'll get back the control in our life.

Make no mistake. Anytime we blame anyone or anything for what is happening in our lives, we are giving away all our power.
SUSAN JEFFERS

16 The shadow and the shame

One of the things that I learned from Ruth was that we all have a 'shadow' self, part of us that is buried inside where we have shoved any feelings we thought would be unacceptable – aspects of our inner lives that we are often unaware of. Some people want to call their shadow their 'soul' or their 'spirit' or their 'Inner Child', and these are all aspects of the part of us that is unconscious.

The original idea of the shadow came from Jung, a man who worked with Freud but came to disagree with him on some fundamental issues.

Although there are some difficult bits within our shadow, things that we might be ashamed of, what I learned from Ruth was that we need to make friends with our shadow and learn from it.

Feeling the shame

At first, when I tried to get to know my shadow, all I could think of was that this buried bit of me must be very bad.

We're back to shame again – the shame chains must be very thick and difficult to break. We say things such as:

• I know I'm not as good as other people.

• I'm a hopeless person – I'll never be able to do what people expect of me.

• If people knew what I was like they wouldn't want to be friends with me.

• I feel dishonest, a fake. I don't know how to be real.

• I'm so bad I think God will reject me.

The sense of shame that we have is not so much about anything that we did; it is about our very selves – who we are.

This is drastic stuff. (But at least we are feeling something! For some survivors that is at least a sign that the zombie-mode is changing.) But believing that at the core of our being we are no good is likely to chain us up even more than we are already. Understanding our shadow is a crucial part of our healing.

Our shadow and what we can learn from it

Yes, there are bits of our shadow that might be 'bad', such as aggression or resentment that we have pushed down because we felt that we were not supposed to show the world our hurt from the abuse. I also think that we try to hide our feelings from ourselves, so we repress them out of fear that we might be left naked and exposed before those we are convinced will reject us.

Our inner core or soul is so much 'us' that we deny the depths of it at our own peril. We can gain a great deal of self-awareness if we focus on our shadow, and that is such a crucial aspect of us changing and becoming more balanced and integrated people. (OK, you might not feel even remotely balanced and integrated but keep going on the chain breaking – you'll get there.)

An example of what I mean by becoming more balanced and integrated is that through personality testing I learned that I was introverted (so I need lots of time on my own), but I've become more balanced and have learned to cope better with being in groups of people.

The more self-knowledge we gain, the more we will be able to change to find peace and joy in our lives. And understanding our shadow is crucial to this.

Accepting our shadow exists

I remember listening to a disc jockey being interviewed on the radio by a psychiatrist and the disc jockey kept on saying, 'What you see is what you get.' He insisted that there was nothing any deeper within him – nothing that he was concealing. The more he denied the depths of his being the funnier it got, but I also became uncomfortable, almost embarrassed for him. As the interview went on it became more and more scary.

None of us is that superficial, I'm quite sure of that. We might like to stay superficial and 'nice', but everyone has 'hidden depths', even when they are not aware of it.

Parts of me are mysterious. This helps me to see that our Great Creator is also deeper and more mysterious than we can ever understand.

We're almost certainly not going to understand our shadow completely, but as a first step, accepting it exists might break one chain.

Sewing our shadow back on

Peter Pan got very upset when his shadow came loose. He needed someone to sew it back on, and like him, if we can learn to live with our shadow as a part of us, we will feel more whole.

Here are some keys to understanding our shadow:

• Feeling and intuition can take more of a role.

• If we feel loved we feel more 'real', more as if we matter as people, and this reduces the sense of shame in our lives.

• Using our feelings and our intuition can give us insight into our soul and some sense of the different 'people' or creatures who are within us.

If you want to find out more about your shadow, you might want to read the books by Steve Shaw and John Monbourquette mentioned in the resources section; but here I want to explain some more of the significance of our shadow and some of the activities we can do to break chains.

Using our intuition

One way to get to know your shadow is to talk to him/her just as you talk and communicate with your Inner Child.

One time to do that is when you sense that something is not quite right – you feel spaced out, or anxious, or you have that general sense of disquiet. I feel that quite a bit, and by stopping and going into dialogue with my spirit, I can get rid of my sense that all is not well.

A few days ago I was puzzled about why I felt so ill at ease. I stopped typing and tried to talk with my spirit. What was wrong?

I knew I needed to be outside in the sunshine to look at the snowdrops, and as I walked down the garden with my little dog, what came through in my dialogue with myself was that an email I'd written had been unnecessarily harsh. I went inside and sent an apology; then I felt fine.

Sometimes I talk to Suzie-doll and Shadow when I'm confused (or to Killer

Whale, who reminds me about my anger and rage – and then the conversation can be much harder to handle). Sometimes big emotions can be bubbling along inside me, so resolving what is going on can take a little longer. Guilt, anger, fear and shame can arise, but so too can joy and delight.

Killer Whale helps me to resolve my anger by letting me know it is there, and accepting that I'm angry inside has become an important aspect of my self-acceptance. We need to accept ourselves just as we are – along with our anger and resentment.

The dialogue we have with ourselves at these times isn't likely to have much to do with left brain logic. It is much more about intuition – a chance for the right brain to come into play and lead us into creative ways of understanding our Inner Self.

Escaping from the shame

One very important thing to say about our shadows is that as you discover yours, I hope you will be able to move away from the sense of shame. OK, we might not be feeling great about our Killer Whale, or the creative thoughts we have about how we might take revenge on our abuser, but there is lots to discover in our shadow that can help us as we try to break free of the effects of abuse.

We learn who we are deep down inside. Hopefully we learn to discard those feelings I listed at the start of the chapter – feeling we aren't good enough and that God and everyone else will reject us.

Every human being on earth has value. What has thrown our inner world into chaos is the abuse. That was not our fault and as you grow and change and break free, I hope that, like me, you will begin to get a sense of your personal value and learn to accept who you are just as you are.

You are a beautiful human person.
PIP WILSON

A strategy for any time when you need to connect with your Inner Self

Hold your non-dominant hand in your dominant hand and tell yourself, 'I'm safe.' If you are not sure what you are feeling, or you are trying to detect something in your shadow, ask yourself, 'What is it that I am feeling?' Touch your Inner Child. The answer is there if you listen.

KEY POINTS

■ Don't be disappointed if you try to dialogue with your soul and nothing seems to happen. The process of communicating effectively with your inner being can take a lifetime. So keep going – and get a cuddly creature to help you.

■ Getting to know our shadows is about learning that life is about joy, not about sadness.

■ We need to accept ourselves and others just as we are.

■ We're 'goodenough'!

CHAIN BREAKING

1. If you haven't already done so, go to a toy shop or a charity shop to find a cuddly creature to help you to understand your soul. Use your intuition. Which creature leaps off the shelf into the arms of your Inner Child?

2. We won't always find great resolution of our moods and thoughts through words. Sometimes we need to draw or paint and I find that this is a comfort when my soul is restless. This 'prayer painting' doesn't need specific, recognizable images – just letting the brush amble across the page in colours that feel right can be reassuring and illuminating. I quite often access anger through prayer painting.

Sometimes I start to feel less stressed when I am meditating in this way, but sometimes I have no idea why – and that doesn't matter. We are all much more complex and mysterious than we can grasp.

3. Try to relax and breathe deeply. Listen to your body. Is there a 'pain in your neck'? What do you feel deeply in your heart at the moment? What's annoying you? Write, paint, draw or play in response to your feelings. You might want to skip in the park or jump on a pile of leaves – it might give the neighbours a bit of a shock but you are becoming the new you, and that matters more than others thinking you have gone away with the fairies.

4. Play can be a great many different things: woodwork; photography; solving those wooden puzzles that you take apart and can spend hours putting back together; sudoku or crossword puzzles; listening and/or dancing to music. The key is to find something we enjoy. Play can open us up to a deeper understanding of who we are.

Remember
You *must* let go of the guilt and shame – that belief that it was all your fault.

You *can* break the chains that try to trap you in the past.

The invitation then is to dance with the shadow.
STEVE SHAW

17 Who am I?
• • • • • • • • • • • • • • • • • • •

I am struck by the number of people I've heard saying that they felt the 'odd one out' in their family, or saying, 'I realized I wasn't like all the other kids in my class.'

I have felt like this all my life about my birth family – I find it really hard to relate to any of them, and they to me.

Thinking about how often this sentiment is expressed, I wonder if there is something about feeling we don't fit in that might be true for most people – or at least for most people from any kind of complicated background?

It could be the logical response of a young person who sees (perhaps with a certain sense of horror) that there is much more to a person than we usually notice in ordinary social interaction. This might be because people are wearing masks (thank goodness for masks so that we can hide our vulnerabilities!), so what we see in someone is not necessarily what they are actually thinking and feeling.

All my life I've felt this terrible guilt. I feel so dirty and ashamed. I knew I was different from everyone else in my family and even when I left home and went to college, I felt an odd one out. I've never had a boyfriend and I don't suppose I ever will. I would have liked to have had kids of my own, but I can't let a man anywhere near me.
SOPHIE

The hidden depths inside everyone
As people discover the depths of themselves from adolescence, through their teenage years and into their twenties, they realize that they have bits of themselves that they want to hide from others. (We tuck these things away as part of our shadow.)

Guilt becomes a big issue. Maybe they wonder if there are these hidden depths in everyone? But there is no way to access these hidden depths – except maybe in close friendships and when we first feel loved, and it is then that we say, 'I feel more loved than I have ever felt before. Now I have found myself.'

Life is difficult

Somehow through our years and years of schooling we were bombarded with thousands of seemingly irrelevant facts about kings and battles and the industrial revolution. But vital skills for surviving life weren't on the curriculum.

• No one told us about depression, or what it feels like to want to harm ourselves.

• No one told us how to handle the thought that life is so awful that suicide feels like a good idea.

Normal life seems impossible – and we are not sure we want 'normal' life anyway because we feel different, shut out, at odds with everyone, even those closest to us. We feel no one understands us. We feel abandoned and utterly alone.

This sense of aloneness could be an aspect of our low self-esteem that we are unaware of, the feeling that:

• we do not quite measure up

• we are failures

• we aren't like other people

• others can manage life but we can't.

Being the scapegoat

This sense of being the 'odd one out' can be emphasized if we were the scapegoat in the family (something I've mentioned before) – a really important concept if you are from a manipulative family.

In my birth family, whatever happened it was my fault! Somehow the others (mother, step-father, older half-brother and younger half-brother) all found ways to put me down and laugh at me. If they could get me to cry or run away, that seemed to bring some sense of balance to the four of them.

Somehow people who are hurting can find a way of putting all the badness that they cannot cope with onto their chosen scapegoat (although they might not be doing it consciously.) Maybe by doing this they don't feel their own badness quite so powerfully and can get some sense of relief from seeing the scapegoat upset or sent out of the fold.

Self-loathing

As I started to write this chapter about self-esteem, I read my journals from years ago and the more I listened to other survivors, and to my own internal voice, I realized that 'low self-esteem' didn't quite express the reality.

The problem is deeper than low self-esteem. It is a deep and clammy self-loathing – self-hatred that we cannot seem to shake off or escape from. It's not 'I don't like myself', as in low self-esteem. It's 'I utterly hate myself, I'm evil and I deserve to die'.

Some Christian survivors thought as I did. If we go to church services our evil selves will pollute everything. So we stay away.

Despising ourselves with such passion is one of our really thick chains, tightly wrapped around our ankles, so it is essential that we address this seriously.

A wonderful truth

This sense of alone-ness, self-loathing and being the 'odd one out' can be terrifying. We even think that our pain can't be communicated to anyone else because it is so powerful and unique to us.

That may well be true. But out of this sense that we are different can come a wonderful healing truth.

We are unique.

We are special.

There is no one like us in the world (even if we are a twin!). Even though my science fiction friends talk of parallel universes and all that kind of thing, I think it is safe to say we are all a 'one off'. So when I found this odd little creature looking at me from a basket of other soft toys, I fell in love with 'it' immediately.

It isn't an anything. It isn't even a he or a she. It is Unique and helps me to remember that I am unique.

Low expectations

For several years I've worked with teachers to improve their classroom practice, and one of the most marked features of schools with low achievement is that the teachers can have low expectations of the children.

But in schools where the head teacher will not allow any adults (teachers, parents, lunchtime supervisors and so on) to say, 'Our children couldn't do that,' the children achieve far more than in schools where expectations are lower. So parents who introduce one of their children as 'my naughty one', will end up with a naughty child. 'Sylvia is our quiet one' silences that child. 'Kevin is our clever one' can make all the other children think they are expected to fail.

What parents and teachers expect is almost always what they get!

If we tell ourselves we can't do something, or that we are 'hopeless', or whatever it is that we have learned to say about ourselves from childhood or have learned as an adult following some kind of abuse, we are putting a ceiling on our achievement that need not be there.

Saying sorry

Another feature of survivors as we talk, or as we keep in touch on-line as a group, is that we are always apologizing. We apologize because:

- we feel bad and want to self-harm, binge, or starve ourselves

- we can't cope with our job, our college course, our family tearing us to pieces

- we can't deal with crowds so we are avoiding shops, church, going out with our mates

- we don't feel we are being a 'goodenough' mother, friend, partner etc.

- we are upset that our doctor, psychiatrist, community psychiatric nurse, carer etc. is losing patience with us

- we are scared of our suicidal thoughts.

None of these things needs an apology. They are quite free of any kind of 'fault' or 'blame'. We are just responding to our circumstances, trying to make sense of those weird feelings and thoughts that overwhelm us.

Lucy: I'm sorry I'm like this.
Sue: Lucy, stop apologizing! You haven't done anything wrong.
Lucy: Sorry.
Sue: You're doing it again. There is no need to say sorry.

Lucy: I'm really sorry.
Sue: You've been through something utterly horrible, so of course you feel
awful. You really don't need to say sorry.
Lucy: Sorry.

I'm fat and ugly

It doesn't actually matter what we look like on the outside, but still I find it hard to look in a mirror. Sometimes when I glimpse myself I see this huge fat monster of a woman and inevitably through my mind goes, 'You look like your mother.' This is something I still cannot deal with. I shudder in disgust sometimes and have to consciously stop myself being so negative towards myself.

I have a poster on my wall of a penguin with little yellow tufty bits coming out of his head and the caption is, 'I was born like this. What's your excuse?'

This makes me laugh – always a good antidote to putting ourselves down.

Raising our self-esteem

If we are to raise our self-esteem and counteract our self-loathing, we need to be very forgiving towards ourselves. It is all too easy if I binge or do something self-destructive to be angry with myself. 'How could you do that you stupid person!'

To raise our self-esteem we need to be aware of how much negative junk we feed back to ourselves, and try to take any failures in our stride. I'm not terribly good at doing that but I'm learning to say, 'Well, I binged today, and I did that because I was stressed with all those people coming to the house and there were lots of biscuits around.'

I think this calmer reaction is more likely to help us be more confident and feel better about ourselves than when we go into a tirade at ourselves about how hopeless we are.

Raising our self-esteem can take a long time, and unless we learn to love and care for ourselves it isn't going to happen.

Understanding our uniqueness

It is as we let ourselves feel loved, held, valued and of huge significance to those around us, and to our Creator, that we can begin to heal ourselves and break free from those chains that grew around us in our years of self-hatred.

It has taken me many years to learn to understand that, and if something difficult happens, I retreat back to my well-known beliefs that it is 'my fault'. 'I'm hopeless.'

But I believe the Great Creator made us out of love, and we can nestle in the arms of this Creator and know that we are loved in all our uniqueness.

So when we feel 'the odd one out', that is because we are the odd one out! We are 'one of a kind'. We are unique. And that is something that can change the whole view we have of ourselves.

Can I break chains?

I can just see you might at this point think, 'Yes, other people can change, but not me. I'm too hopeless. I will always hate myself.'

This is a lie. It is your abuser's voice inside you and you can start to break that chain now.

How do we do that?

By being absolutely determined not to let our abusers continue to have influence on our life.

Here we are at another one of those transforming 'sitting on the end of the bed' moments. Are we going to continue to believe the lies that the abuse was all our fault? That we are evil? That we deserve only bad things in our lives?

No?

Then we can change all those inner thoughts we cling on to.

Here are some suggestions and things that helped me to cut my chains.

Strategies for getting rid of self-loathing

1. Make sure you are monitoring your negative thinking (see the end of chapter five).

2. Learn to reject the family myths that come your way. These can start: 'You always…', 'You're the difficult one', 'Why can you never…?' I used to believe my mother when she said, 'You will never come to anything.' If we can learn gently to challenge ourselves about these lies and myths by writing in our journal, painting or whatever creative activity grabs us, we can learn to change how we think about ourselves.

3. Listen carefully to friends, colleagues and family to see if you are their scapegoat – do they put onto you all the 'badness' to help

themselves to feel better? This kind of 'blame shifting' is ever so common. People seem to do it all the time and we need to recognize it and reject the burden that people put on us.

4. I've noticed that complimenting people can lead to a greater sense of valuing myself. If we take time to thank people, or to give them positive feedback about something, they respond positively – and that affects the person who gave the compliment. (This strategy works well for teachers with difficult kids.)

KEY POINTS

■ Low self-esteem is common among survivors.

■ We can change our self-esteem and self-loathing.

■ What we look like on the outside doesn't matter. It is who we are inside that matters.

CHAIN BREAKING

1. Write or draw about your thoughts as you read this chapter. If that is hard, try to complete these sentences:
    'The lies I'm told include…'
    'The family put their junk onto me by…'
    'I think my abuser/s have some control over me still because I…'

2. We can set out on a deliberate plan to be kinder to ourselves. For example, I'm really beating myself up at the moment about my bingeing and chaotic eating. But the more I say to myself, 'You are hopeless,' the worse I feel so the more I eat! I think if I was to be kinder to myself and concentrate more on enjoying exercise rather than obsessing about food, I'd probably relax more, value myself more and therefore look after myself better.
    Write *'I could be kinder to myself by…'*
    (Yes, you *do* deserve it!)

3. One aspect of being kinder to ourselves is to cherish and nurture our body more – long slow baths with relaxing oil, joining a keep fit class and so on. You could choose one small manageable thing to do this week.
    'This week I will…'

4. Write with your non-dominant hand to your Inner Child. 'How are you feeling today?'

5. We need to find ways to take the first faltering steps towards learning to love ourselves. That can seem impossible at first. Love myself? Surely not. But it is as we learn to love and care for ourselves that we will get the strength we need to break free of the chains of abuse.

We can:

❖ do our best to look after our physical bodies through healthy eating, exercise, putting cream on our skin etc.

❖ spend time doing things that we *like* doing, not always making ourselves do things because we feel we *should* do them. Hobbies such as enjoying films etc. are important for our wellbeing and for developing our self-esteem.

Remember

We can learn to love ourselves – though it might take time, effort and probably lots of tears along the way.

We do change! That's the whole point of reading this book. We can break the chains. We can set ourselves free.

But it takes time.

You are a marvel. You are unique.
PABLO CASALS

18 Why do I switch off?

If I can't cope with some emotional pain I switch off. Even if someone is just telling me something very ordinary that I don't think I need to know, I switch off. In fact, I have switching off down to a fine art, in a whole range of circumstances and at a whole range of levels, and I see other survivors doing it too.

And that is absolutely OK.

But if we are really to work through the pain, I mean really do it, then we need to learn to allow ourselves to engage our head, heart, mind, soul, Inner Child, 'hidden' memories and emotions – all of ourselves – in this process.

I don't think we are made up of lots of bits really; we are actually a 'whole' person. But one way or another, I think, if we are great at switching off, we have learned to 'split'. That's the only way I can describe it.

Switching off is a great survival mechanism, but we also have to learn to 'switch on' if we are to break the chains whose existence we are adamantly denying. Our whole person must come into play and I find I have to concentrate terribly hard to be sure I'm 'all there'. I have to take loads of time to consider just one thing (see the word wall activity at the end of this chapter). I have to talk myself through the emotional implications of something if I know I'm switched off emotionally.

Suzie Penguin helps me with this. She had to 'switch off' in the cold Antarctic winter when there was no food – she switched off to survive. I find that holding her soft body helps me to stay 'in the present' – what some people call being 'grounded'.

Unpacking the hurts

It is as if we have to unpack the hurts to get them out of our mind, where they lurk ominously waiting to jump out on us when we least expect them.

- We have to look at the hurt to know our honest reaction to it and to assess how that hurt is influencing us (usually for the worse).

- We need to let our Inner Child weep and/or rage and storm for that hurt child – or the adult – that was so abused.

- Once we have allowed ourselves to see the truth of that hurt, we then need to be determined to recover – to break those chains that would hold us to that hurt and impair our present life.

Yes, someone might tell us we are 'wallowing in it' if we take a long time to get to 'recovery', but if we stick determinedly to our aim of breaking those chains that bind us, this process of 'uncovery' will in the end lead to recovery.

Finding truth
It is truth that will set us free in the end and part of that truth is that healing can take a very long time – a lifetime maybe? That feels realistic to me.

Those of us who have indistinct early memories may never come to know much more truth than that 'something happened'.

One aspect of letting truth shine into our memories is to be aware when we are switching off, and if it is appropriate, to try to find out why we are switching off. What are we trying to avoid? Usually it is some kind of emotion or thought that we can't quite deal with. Learning not to switch off at that point can sometimes give us clearer memories.

> *The knowledge of horrible events periodically intrudes into public awareness but it is rarely retained for long. Denial, repression and dissociation operate on a social as well as an individual level.*
> JUDITH HERMAN

Understanding switching off
Probably everyone switches off in some situations, such as during a boring meeting, or while sitting on the bus planning the evening meal. We can become oblivious to what is going on around us.

'Dissociation' is the general term for this 'switching off', but again, this term is used in daily life for 'ordinary' things, which are nothing to do with abuse. Runners talk of dissociating, because we switch off to distract ourselves in a long run. It's better to listen to music or to watch the television in the gym than it is to think about the next three hours of the run. But we must 'associate' in some circumstances, such as if we are going over uneven ground and we want to avoid an ankle injury.

Inner personalities

Some survivors have an awareness of more than one Inner Child, or 'person' within them, so their switching can be:

- from one of their 'inner personalities' to another

- one of their 'inner people' becoming 'triggered out' and unable to respond appropriately

- one of their 'inner people' taking control, influencing what is happening but without being completely in control (obviously this is confusing for everyone concerned)

- one of their 'people' being triggered, but somehow keeping complete control over both their thinking and the physical body – but 'they' can do nothing about it.

Any of these can result in total chaos!

But these events don't need to be anything to panic about. Of course we find them disconcerting, especially when we have no clear memory of what happened. There are some web and other references to find support for our dissociating in the resources section, and this 'changing personalities' is something you might want to talk about in a self-help group.

I've become aware of a little boy inside me as well as my little Inner Child girl and this is perfectly normal. But even if you aren't aware of more than one Inner Child, you might recognize in yourself a sense of 'becoming a different person', perhaps for a woman before her period. I know I can change quickly and sometimes disastrously from 'Sue the smiley mother and happy teacher' into 'Sue who can't cope, who doesn't make eye contact and who cuts off all communication'. I become 'Sue the zombie' and I'm unreliable and unpredictable, two common features of survivors.

It's as if some trigger invades our senses and we change channels like a television set. It is so very hard to change back to 'normal' because we lose a sense of what that is.

Levels of switching off

We can be switched off in varying degrees of intensity.

1. The first level is the totally normal thing to do when we go into our own thoughts for various reasons. We switch off not through stress, but because we want to think.

2. 'Freaking out' is a phrase I use when something has happened to upset me – something has 'triggered' some bad memory or feeling. I go into 'aaauugghhh' mode and for a while I feel I can't cope. So in a restaurant or on a plane, a man near me wiggling his leg would be likely to result in me needing to escape.

   When I'm freaked out I do have complete control of what is going on. I try to manage my emotions. I know what is happening and I'm trying to be OK.

3. What I call 'spacing out' is when we dissociate at a slightly deeper level, so we have a greater loss of touch with reality. I do this a lot, though much less than I used to.

   I talked to a few survivors about this and we felt that sometimes we have some difficulty coming back from this state. That's how it is for me. I tend not to be able to hear or even be aware of what is going on around me until I switch back.

4. There is a deeper kind of dissociation – a losing touch with reality, time, the people around you and so on – that mostly I don't do now. It is scary and difficult to deal with. It can be a huge problem for survivors, especially if they feel they have no control over what is happening, and if they lose the memory of what they did while they were dissociating.

Talking to David about this I said, 'Of course I don't do this "deep dissociating" now where I can't remember what happened.'

'Yes you do,' he said.

That shook me. I was so sure I never did that now, but I can see that under extreme pressure I could be doing it – but without realizing. As we talked about it I came to see that what I thought never happened had been happening very occasionally, but somehow I was cutting those times out of my conscious memory.

At its very worst, this deep dissociating can become so bad that the person is in a catatonic state. I saw this often in people when I was in mental hospitals, and David says that in the past I've been like that too. The person is left with little or no memory of what happens and they are so far out of touch with reality that they may be put in hospital long term. (Recent research reveals that many people in long stay mental hospitals have been abused.)

I was given all kinds of medication when I was in hospital and mostly that made me passive and I behaved like a zombie. Some of that giving of medication was abusive – I was made to take it when I didn't want to – because in one case I felt so ill on it and knew that it was making me hallucinate.

While I see that staff in mental hospitals must be safe and that they must use drugs available to them to be safe, I felt that in my experience and that of others, medication was used to benefit the staff – and one outcome of being given far too much tranquillizer was to stop us *feeling* anything.

Of course outbursts of emotion could be difficult on a ward of unstable people, and if we are dissociating and having flashbacks and things there is the potential for difficulties. But I am constantly amazed when I look back on those admissions to hospital that no doctor or nurse ever seemed to get close to what was going on inside me.

But these were mostly the days before my memories returned so I didn't know either what was going on inside me. I had no idea why my drive to be dead was so powerful.

I think I spent days dissociating and doing the zombie thing. As a way of passing time that was fine, but in terms of working through the pain it was a bit of a disaster.

Strategies for dealing with switching off

If we are starting to panic, or feeling we are starting to dissociate and we don't want to (it might not be safe to do so where we are), we must have some strategies ready. (At home we can curl up in our bed, or sit and listen to our Inner Child.)

1. It's important to try to come back to the present and to get ourselves to a safe place. If it isn't possible to escape (we're on a crowded train, for example) then we need to learn strategies that will help us to endure what is happening.

2. You can hold your own hand. Hold your right (or dominant) hand

around your non-dominant hand – as if you were holding the hand of a child. You can think of this as protecting your Inner Child who is frightened.

3. Listen really carefully to the sounds around you. This can help you to come back into the present and into the place where you are, so stopping your mind from switching off.

4. Try to identify what your Inner Child wants. I find this hard when I'm freaking out, but I can see how it is useful to know that I could rescue myself by connecting with my Inner Child.

5. If you are finding that you are dissociating and not remembering large chunks of time, you do need to tell a doctor or a supporter about that. It might be helpful to plan what to do if you can predict your dissociating, or to talk with a supporter about what they can best do – such as not let you out if you might be vulnerable outside the home.

KEY POINTS

■ Unpacking the pain can be costly, take a long time, and be emotionally upsetting.

■ Denying the strength of our hurts is only likely to make recovery a much longer process.

■ We must allow ourselves to work through the pain, not ignore it. We need to find out what those chains are that hold us down.

■ Dissociation is normal but can lead to us being unreliable and unpredictable.

■ Switching off is fine as a survival mechanism, but in the end we must learn to switch on to deal with our inner pain.

■ Getting to know our Inner Child or Children is important for our healing.

CHAIN BREAKING

1. Write/draw/paint/dance your switching off. What can you learn from what you wrote/drew?

Santa Clara County Library District

408-293-2326

Checked Out Items 9/5/2019 19:38
XXXXXXXXXX0385

Item Title	Due Date
1. Breaking the chains of abuse : a practical guide 33305212967446	9/26/2019
2. Your daughter's bedroom : insights for raising confident women 33305223560107	9/26/2019

No of Items: 2

24/7 Telecirc: 800-471-0991
www.sccl.org
Thank you for visiting our library.

2. Do you know what triggers you to switch off? Can you commit to recording in some way your thinking as you start to switch off so you can identify your triggers?

3. There are some resources in the back of the book to help with dissociating.

4. You might be overloading yourself with too many different ideas as you try to break your chains. Can you identify just one idea you would like to focus on? Maybe it could be a trigger you want to understand, or working at your frustrations with spacing out, or something else that has arisen as you read this book.

When I feel this sense of overload I do a 'word wall' activity. I draw a brick wall on paper and put just my key word (such as 'triggers') on one of the bricks and stick the paper up where I will see it. Gradually I add words onto the other bricks as I discover other words or ideas that relate to my key word. After a few weeks or months I try to sit for a while and write or draw in my journal to focus my thoughts. Once when I did this I realized with some astonishment how much I'm triggered by smells, particularly deodorant and after-shave.

Remember

Dissociating, freaking out and all the rest of this way of behaving are perfectly normal among people who have been traumatized. It is just our body trying to cope with the trauma – something might have happened that our inner world couldn't cope with at that moment so our body closes down in order to cope.

That's OK. That is how we are managing life at this time.
It will get better.

I hadn't so much forgot as I couldn't bring myself to remember. Other things were more important.
MAYA ANGELOUS

Puff the Puffin

Part 5

Starting to heal

· ·

This section is about the healing and freedom we can find as we begin to break our chains. As we work our way through building our self-esteem and struggling free of the guilt and shame, some days we find ourselves smiling more, finding a sense of lightness in our being.

We are starting to heal!

We begin to find the energy to consider our anger and start to find ways of letting go of our resentments.

We still trip over our chains, but we've set our mind on healing. Whatever it takes we're going to keep going.

It is never too late to be what you might have been.

GEORGE ELIOT

19 Healing with puffins

Many people seem to have a 'worst thing' about themselves or about their lives that they would like to see changed. Mine was going into total collapse sometimes when people criticized me. But now I know I am much stronger, and I have strategies for dealing with my 'worst thing'.

Some of my new ability to take some criticisms (sometimes!) is simply one aspect of getting older and, hopefully, wiser.

For many survivors, aspects of trust can be their 'worst thing'. So probably our trust in ourselves is constantly changing – hopefully growing stronger as our self-esteem and confidence grow.

It is then that we start to see more clearly that we are healing.

Puffin joins in

When I stopped teaching, David and I began to take holidays in May and one of our favourite places to go was the island of Skomer off the South Wales coast.

Like thousands of people, my favourite bird is a puffin. I adore them and have pictures of them all over the place – on my key ring, jumpers and even shopping bags. So part of the Skomer trips was to get close to puffins and enjoy time just sitting watching them dive for fish and bring them to their burrows for their baby, dodging marauding skuas on the way.

Looking for peace

As I struggled to find healing from the nightmares, phobias and depression, my times away bird-watching were always times to re-evaluate life – to stand back and see where I was going and what my hopes, dreams and ambitions were.

There is something about sitting on a cliff among the sea-pink flowers that to me means peace and contentment, and as I sat looking at the puffins one came really near to me and I watched it, thrilled to get such a close view.

As I watched this beautiful creature, it felt as if the stress and trauma of my life was ebbing away – melting into insignificance.

It felt as if from nowhere the thought came that, because of a puffin, the rest of the world with its wars and difficulties mattered less.

Moving on

Watching the puffin I realized I could move on from some of the hurts. The stress and the depression mattered less because there were puffins.

There will always be puffins – if we can get our act together to preserve the planet for our children and their children. And somehow the very thought that these delightful little birds exist was something that filled me with peace and joy that day.

It was one of those transforming moments, a time to realize that I could break the chains – I could fight free – I could move on into a better phase in my life, free of resentments, free of all the memories of abuse that were holding me in a state of fear.

So Puff the Puffin came to join the creatures. He helps me to hope for a better tomorrow and he also teaches me about peace and joy.

Healing by laughing

Laughter can get us going towards that deep kind of joy we sometimes feel when we find that all is well with the world. I hope you get glimpses of that as I do.

Laughing is very good. It has been shown to bring healing by lifting us out of phases of stress and burnout, relieving depression and releasing endorphins in our body that make us feel happy.

There is no quick fix, but there are lots of funny programmes on the television and radio, and plenty of funny books.

Trusting ourselves and beginning to feel we are healing can be kick started by humour.

Re-touching

Healing from the effects of abuse involves us needing to 'touch' the same areas time after time. We know, for example, that it wasn't our fault – but then something happens and we go back to believing it *was* our fault.

We take on board strategies for helping us deal with flashbacks. Then we get another flashback and we can feel we are back where we were a year ago and have to re-learn the strategies all over again.

This could tend to make us feel stupid, or hopeless. We feel that we fail even at our own healing, but what is going on is a well-known part of life – we have to 'touch' the same idea over and over again.

That is why the helix is such a powerful model when it comes to

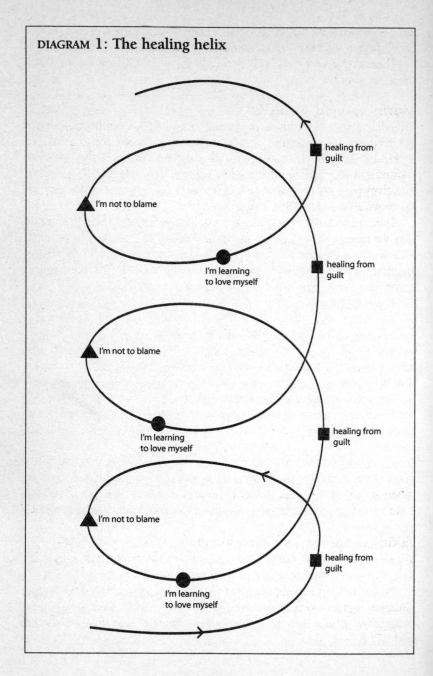

DIAGRAM 1: The healing helix

healing from guilt

healing from guilt

I'm not to blame

I'm learning to love myself

I'm not to blame

I'm learning to love myself

healing from guilt

I'm not to blame

healing from guilt

I'm learning to love myself

almost any area of human life – and a helix is part of the structure of our DNA, fundamental to understanding human life.

This is how it is as we heal from abuse. We need to keep revisiting the same thing.

Moving around the helix

This diagram shows what is happening. (It's hugely simplified – I can't get every aspect of healing written on it.) As we learn, for example, to be kind to ourselves, we grasp the idea and tell ourselves that we have learned something: beating ourselves up gets us nowhere; being kind to ourselves pays off by giving us good feelings; we have a good day, we know we are not to blame and so on.

Then we face the next difficult bit of life, perhaps someone telling us that we need to 'forgive and forget and move on'. For the hundredth time we try to smile and say 'mmm', hoping the person will take this as agreement, but allowing ourselves the space to feel that forgiving is easier said than done – and forgetting is an impossibility.

The guilt hits us.

We touch the healing from guilt aspect again and we remind ourselves again that we need to dump the guilt.

We go back to lessons we learned months ago. It's OK for now not to feel forgiving. It's OK. Months or years later we are likely to touch that bit of the helix again.

We do need to grasp that this is a perfectly normal way of living our life. Everyone needs to come back to the same things over and over again – those things that are the foundation of human growth towards maturity.

It's *normal* to need to keep revisiting each aspect of healing. So when you've read through this book, to need to come back again and again to different bits of the helix would be expected. That's how we break the chains – not in any set order or way but in an order that is unique to us.

Taking our setbacks with good grace

We must keep at the front of our mind that there really is no quick fix. The chains that we broke last year might seem to have come back.

Probably what has happened is that we are facing the same learning situation again – but at a higher level on the helix. We have made progress, even if it feels as if we now have more chains than we started with.

The chains *are* fewer. We *are* breaking them. We just need to learn to take our setbacks as part of the normal processes of life.

We are 'goodenough'.

We are getting better.

We just had a setback – everyone gets them.

Learning to face our setbacks with good grace is a life skill in itself.

KEY POINTS

■ It can be helpful to identify one or more of our 'worst things'.

■ Laughter can be healing.

■ There is no quick fix.

■ Healing can involve us in coming back again and again to the same thing.

■ Expect setbacks.

CHAIN BREAKING

1. Make a date with yourself in your diary for a laughing time. Probably if you don't pre-plan it you won't do it – so plan it!

2. How can you build up your store of funny things? Visit charity shops to look for discarded videos? Make a regular date with yourself to watch favourite comedians on television?

3. Write or draw about the ways you are challenging your negative thinking. (If you are like me you are probably still nagging yourself with negative thoughts. Work at getting rid of them!)

4. I find that my journal helps me to keep tabs on my progress, so it is important to write when we are feeling good. This can then be something we can read on the harder days. As the saying goes, 'Nothing breeds success like success.' Focus on the good times – they give us hope.

Look back in your journal/folder of drawings and give yourself a gold star sticker everywhere you can see you've broken a chain.

5. Write/draw/dance your feelings about healing.

Remember

The effects of abuse can be long term but they don't need to be permanent.

> *The big question is whether you are going to be able to say a hearty yes to your adventure.*
>
> JOSEPH CAMPBELL

20 Beginning to feel angry

For as long as I can remember I've always been intrigued by anger, particularly as a young adult when I realized that in some families showing any anger wasn't the done thing – there was a great deal of 'sweeping it under the carpet'. In my family of origin, when either of my parents were angry, they were usually violent as well. I noticed that if I expressed anger I got beaten up. So it seems natural that I would be frightened of anger or any kind of conflict.

I've also found people who say that their families didn't display much anger, but still those people can be afraid of anger because they are not used to it and it freaks them out.

Mostly anger has been a 'no go' area for me. I buried my angry feelings, and no doubt it was this rage within me that was part of the repeated depressed phases I experienced.

However, working with Ruth I was beginning to *feel* angry – just a tiny bit and only for fleeting moments. But I knew I was starting to feel quite a bit of rage for my uncle, and I found that terrifying.

I felt blank about Ernie my step-father – I think in some ways I was still afraid of him. He'd been dead for many years but here I was saying all these really bad things about him, and I think I almost expected him to come and beat me up.

What if he is in heaven and can see and hear me now? Would I be shut out of heaven for being so wicked? Could someone who was so aggressive and cruel be allowed to go to heaven? Even when he openly said that everything to do with religion was rubbish?

I was still afraid that I was making it all up.

Letting anger out

The first time I was really aware of being angry – letting it all leap out of my mouth – was when my older half-brother rang me up and started yelling at me about how I wasn't looking after our mother well enough. (She was in a nursing home dying of liver cancer.)

I was in a total rage! I went to see our mother at least once a week, sometimes twice or three times, driving right across London (which was often two hours each way), and he hadn't visited our mother in two years.

Wow! I really let him have it. I yelled louder than he did. I turned everything he said back onto him. I told him that there were other members of the family listening to what we were saying. (My son and daughter-in-law were incredibly startled at my yelling, but I thought I was behaving in a way suitable for the occasion.) I made him back down and told him that our mother continually asked for him and said to me, 'The only one of my children I've ever loved is Angus.'

'But you don't go to see her,' I said. 'How do you think she feels about that?'

I most definitely won the argument. He still didn't go to see her for several months and by the time he did go, our mother had lapsed into unconsciousness and was an almost unrecognizable ghostly skeleton, and it was clear from my brother's face that he was deeply shocked as he walked into her room.

So he never got to say his goodbye and she died a few days later as I sat beside her.

Anger is frightening

I trembled for hours after that phone call with my brother. I was pleased with myself both for standing up to him and for refusing to accept his criticism (that everything was my fault!), but I was also afraid of what I had done.

I'd startled my two young family members who were listening to me yell. I'd startled myself when the anger had just burst out of me. I realized that if my brother had actually been there in front of me I'd have behaved differently. If he'd turned up at my house and I'd been on my own I could never have stood up for what I thought was right. (It was one of my nightmares that one of my brothers would turn up and beat me up or stab me.)

So I'd turned over a lifetime habit for both of us – him (with the rest of my family) putting everything bad onto me (so no one else had to take responsibility), and me, having been the 'victim' so long, too weak to stand up for myself, now standing up for justice.

I was shocked at the amount of anger within me, and when I talked it all through with Ruth I was aware that I didn't really want any more anger to come out if it was going to be so terrifying. (But at the same time I was beginning to be secretly more and more pleased at what I'd said and done to my brother!)

Is it OK to be angry?

I've been told that as a Christian I 'shouldn't get angry'. This is weird because Jesus was angry – he got really het up about people selling things in the temple and he took a whip and drove those people out – real Indiana Jones stuff!

Wow – that's anger!

But over and over again in newspapers and on television we see people assuming that Christians should be meek and mild all the time and any kind of standing up for justice or whatever is condemned.

In my head I know that is stupid. Jesus did talk about love and meekness, but at no point did he teach the 'just-walk-all-over-me' stuff.

But I realized that with my fear of showing anger, and my wish to be a loving and caring person, I seemed to have taken on board the whole notion that anger is 'bad' and sweeping it under the carpet out of sight is 'good'. At least that might be one explanation of why I felt numb. And why my outburst with my brother resulted in me being frightened of the small amount of anger I was beginning to feel about my uncle.

I feel dead inside

So many survivors say they feel dead inside. We go around in zombie mode – feel nothing, then it won't hurt. This can be seen as a kind of dissociating in which we cut off from the reality of the pain inside us. We cannot cope with the overwhelming feelings so we look for other coping strategies.

But our anger churns away inside us, even when we try so hard to ignore it, and for some of us the deadened anger can burst out in the form of some kind of self-harming. I'm often alarmed to find that when I've been feeling dead inside and I binge on food in a serious way, it is as if I have no control over my life for a while. When it is all over, I can't quite believe what I've done. It is as if a different person in me did the eating and I was too spaced out and dead inside to do anything about it.

But at least it brings an end to the sense of numbness.

Sometimes I self-injure to make myself feel something because I'm just totally numb. Other times I cut to make myself numb because I can't deal with what I'm feeling. I mostly do it when I'm angry. Maybe I was raised not to be angry, or show anger. But whenever I'm mad, I find myself to be at fault, so

The Ernie Monster

One day, in my deadened state, I went to the local art and craft shop and bought some pink and purple felt and some Velcro (that sticky fastening tape that you can rip open with a satisfying tear) and set about making The Ernie Monster. I'm not sure why I made him – even now I don't quite know why I gave up several hours to make him. Maybe it was because I have this belief that when we are creative we are at our most God-like, or maybe I wanted the experience of containing this violent man whom I had no other way of communicating with because he was dead.

But maybe I made it because of his detachable penis and nose. I loved yanking his penis off with a teeth-grinding tearing sound – that was so healing. (I had a big fear of noses, so people wanting to greet me with a kiss were freaking me out. I couldn't even cope with David kissing me sometimes, which we both found upsetting – but that was how it was at the time.)

I took The Ernie Monster to show Ruth and demonstrated how to rip off the nose and penis. Her reaction was so wonderful I just had to take Monster to the survivors' group I went to at the time. There was one man there and he took my demonstration of ripping off the penis with good grace!

I told Ruth a few weeks later that I felt nothing for Ernie. No anger. Nothing.

'But The Ernie Monster shows you are angry inside,' she said.

Yes. I had to agree with her. I felt nothing. But I had made my anger into a stuffed toy. I'd sewn anger. I began to see that it could be my way of being creative about my inner anger that was out of reach.

So I learned that anger can be expressed in many different ways. We

165

don't have to shout and storm and break things. We can feel anger quietly.

One of the ways of expressing anger I was using extensively at the time was writing letters that I never sent. I wrote mostly to my mother, but sometimes to my brothers.

Protecting people

The Ernie Monster isn't, of course, allowed anywhere near my other creatures. They all have to be safe. The Monster has to sit in the bottom of a cupboard, enclosed in a plastic bag, and the only things that go near him are shoes.

Of course we feel angry at the thought that an abuser might well prowl around looking for new victims, but also we feel fear – rightly. Speaking out can be dangerous. Always take advice and talk to supporters before you say anything publicly about your abusers, because it can be a dangerous thing to do. Of course we want to speak out, like Helen in the introduction did on her T-shirt. But always consider first the protection of you and your family if you intend to 'tell'.

Anger can lead to justice

People I have known who have gone to court have done so well – their bravery astounds me. I know that it can be hard just to tell family about abuse, so going to court seems devastatingly difficult. There are many stories in various books about sexual abuse – older children trying to protect younger ones from an abusive parent, cousins speaking out to protect others from the same ordeal they went through, even patients speaking out about abusive doctors.

A dear friend of mine was unsure about whether she could join other women from her village in giving evidence about many instances of sexual abuse when they were children. The abuser was a man who was a well-known children's writer so it would get publicity. Of course she was unsure if she could cope.

In the end she did give evidence, and her face as she told her story showed some of the stress of what she had been through, but also the peace and joy of having stood up for justice. They won their case – one less abuser on the loose. One more message to abusers: 'Look out! Survivors are starting to find a voice – we don't need to be silent any longer.'

KEY POINTS

■ The ways in which we react to anger and conflict are likely to be linked to our earlier experiences.

■ It is possible to express our anger when that is appropriate.

■ It can be hard to detect our anger.

■ Appropriate anger can be good and healing.

BREAKING CHAINS

1. Finish this sentence: *'I remember being angry when…'*

If you're not ready to write that sentence you could stick the words up where you will see them – maybe put them on a sticky note in your diary and move it from page to page as the weeks go by. Gradually you may find you do remember some times of feeling angry.

2. How was anger expressed in those around you when you were a child? Can you link that with your inner feelings now?

'When I was a child anger was shown…'
'I think that means now that I…'

3. Draw or paint anger. Or make a monster.

Remember

Survivors of any kind of abuse can appear calm and happy on the outside but be full of rage and hostility on the inside. That seems to be 'normal' for survivors.

Wanting revenge is understandable and normal – but don't act it out!

Anger is an emotion of self-protection… When anger or rage becomes chronic in the wake of trauma, difficulties can emerge in an individual's daily life. Inappropriate or misdirected anger can interfere with interpersonal relationships and job stability, provoking others to anger can become a danger in itself. How many instances of 'road rage', for example, are incited by a short temper that has its roots in unresolved trauma?
BABETTE ROTHSCHILD

21 Understanding anger

Whatever was I going to do if angry feelings came bursting out into the open unexpectedly and unpredictably?

The only thing I could think of was to work it out through creatures. I already had Killer Whale and then I found Wolf. She is soft and cuddly, but well known for her killer instinct and night-time howling that puts fear into those who can hear her. That was exactly right – I wanted the cuddly side of her as well as her instinct to kill.

I would hug Wolf and talk to her, and write about her in my journal.

Reading that now I can see that what I was trying to do back then was make my anger more acceptable. I believed in my head that it was OK to feel anger, but still I felt guilty and confused as increasingly it looked as if I was going to have to admit not just to anger inside me, but pent-up, potentially explosive rage and a deep hatred of my abusers. In some weird way I'd convinced myself that I was wrong to feel this hatred. Shouldn't I try to love everyone?

But I came to see that the opposite of love is not hatred but indifference. It was normal to hate my abusers. I discovered I both loved and hated my mother at the same time.

Yet most of the time I still felt dead inside – no sense of anger at all. I'd ask myself, 'Are you angry with Ernie?'

I felt nothing. I didn't know if this was because I'd already forgiven him and the anger had evaporated as a result, or if I wasn't yet able to feel the anger for some reason.

Anger is one of the most difficult emotions that human beings face.
CARROLL SAUSSY

Anger and fear

Lots of us are frightened by our anger: what will happen if I let it out? We can fear any kind of conflict – when honest feelings might come out and we feel we could be hurt emotionally and even physically. I felt dreadful fear when I was working with Ruth. If I let my anger out, she might disappear in some cataclysmic explosion that I caused.

But there can be another thing behind our fear of anger – that if I'm angry and say so, you might reject me, you won't like me. And so many of us live on the edge of the fear that when people really get to know us inside they will walk away from us.

Honesty too can be feared. If we say what we really think you might reject us, so we keep our true thoughts and feelings under cover. That might not always be the best thing to be doing – we could just be dodging an issue that needs to be faced.

Having said that though, there are often times when it is best to hide our true feelings. There are trivial things like a friend's awful new dress – best just to smile and make the non-committal 'mmm' sound!

But there are more serious things, such as relationships within families, when it is wise and sensible to keep some thoughts to ourselves. Speaking out just might make everything worse.

…healthy anger can be defined as a response to the experience of being ignored, trivialized, or rejected, or as an empathic response to the witnessing of someone else being ignored, injured, trivialized or rejected.
CARROLL SAUSSY

Putting anger onto the wrong person
One thing that comes through clearly in any book about anger is our tendency to put our anger onto the wrong person. For example, if I feel angry with the woman in the shop who is completely unhelpful, but: I don't express my frustration to her; or I don't realize what is going on with my anger and deal with it; or I don't put my emotions back together with sufficient self-awareness… then I might go home and be angry with David.

When my step-father beat up my mother, she would often be angry with me for no reason – other than that it might have helped her, I suppose, to deal with her confused feelings about The Monster she had married.

Anger is complex stuff
For survivors the complexities are compounded by the following things.

- we bury the memories of abuse

- we fear our abusers

- we are trying to recover from Post-Traumatic Stress Disorder

- the world wants to keep us silent

- we're told to 'forgive and forget', and

- no one seems to understand why we harm ourselves, have eating problems and sometimes feel suicidal.

Expressing our anger in the right way to the right person as well as dealing with all that lot is a bit mind-numbing.

> *Anger is a complex emotion, of which fear is often a significant component…*
> *Expressing anger or being on the receiving end of it can be particularly*
> *complex in relationships of unequal power… Fear of rejection or criticism*
> *often inhibits a person from getting angry… [and others may experience] fear*
> *of being perceived as uncaring or even abusive. However, if angry feelings are*
> *suppressed without addressing their underlying cause, the risk is that anger*
> *leaks out in passive-aggressive behaviour or erupts at an inappropriate time.*
> KATE LITCHFIELD

Anger in disguise

One of the most frequently mentioned things in books about anger is that we express anger in lots of different ways and often we might not see these things as anger. Depression is the most obvious disguise anger takes on, so many people say that depression is anger turned inwards on ourselves.

Yes. That makes sense. Just as our chaotic eating and our self-harming are things we do to cope with our inner feelings, so anger comes out from where we bury it in sometimes unexpected ways.

Physical illnesses such as headaches and maybe high blood pressure can be about unexpressed anger, and some writers claim that it can also cause a wider range of physical illnesses.

I'm pretty sure that over- or under-eating can be anger in disguise. When I get feelings I can't understand or am frightened of, I 'comfort eat'. If I cover my anger with layers of chocolate brownies, the anger is less scary and my thoughts will get distracted first by the wonder and delight of the brownies (note the plural there) and then even more by my guilt and rage for pigging out and thwarting my plans to be thin and beautiful by next month.

I can keep this annoyance with myself going for hours, by which time I've completely obscured the feelings I couldn't cope with in the first place. So these feelings go deep inside me, where I think they lurk until something else triggers them and they leap up at me again.

This is my argument for why I cannot give up chocolate – it would be too stressful. I need it!

What's under the anger?

One of the things that is really intriguing in books about anger is the thought that anger is a secondary emotion – another emotion is always underneath it. So if we are really brave, the thing to do is to look at what is really going on under the anger. The possibilities could include:

- the sense that someone has violated our boundaries

- feeling that someone has rejected us (or we think they have)

- feeling vulnerable and powerless (being near our abuser/s or in a situation that reminds us in some way of the abuse)

- expecting something to happen and then it doesn't – so we feel deeply let down and disappointed

- knowing we have to keep quiet about the abuse and anything else even remotely connected with it (not saying what we really feel when family are around us, for example), so we feel we have no voice and are not allowed to be our True Self.

In other words, our feelings of anger are about some deep pain we have inside us, a pain that maybe we don't know how to express – possibly because we tried to express it once and we were put down and not listened to. Or possibly because we are still in the grip of the secrecy our abuser stuck onto us with superglue.

Anger is OK

Anger is a basic emotion and every human being is bound to experience it at some time in their life: watch toddlers playing together – they do

171

the anger thing very well. They just grab the toy back when it is taken with a straightforward angry look. They know exactly what they feel.

It's OK to feel angry!

It's an emotion, not a crime.

But what is not so good is expressing our anger in a way that could hurt someone.

However, it is common amongst survivors to want actually to harm our abusers – and even to harm others who aren't abusive, but we still feel angry with them. Obviously this boiling, pent-up rage can be a big problem – and it is very worrying for our supporters.

Expressing anger

At a workshop I was leading about sexual abuse, one of the counsellors on the course suggested to me that it's not a good idea to do things like jumping on cans to crush them and kicking a football furiously as I had suggested. She said that it is now thought that these kinds of angry actions can actually make the inner anger worse. (Presumably she meant that it was best to deal with anger in calmer and less violent ways.)

I found this most intriguing and set about asking people over the next few weeks what their view on that was. Opinion was divided. For myself, I think that jumping on cans and furiously digging the garden can be hugely therapeutic, but I notice I rarely actually do those things. It's good just to *think* I do it and keep it in reserve for the days when rage takes me over.

But I can see how people might think kicking or stabbing a cushion to death could make the anger worse, because the anger would be out there and could be seen.

But is that really worse?

Isn't it more real? And wouldn't that be a good thing?

Knots of rage

I think that letting a knot of rage build up inside us, which is getting increasingly difficult to unravel, would be much worse than the odd bit of leaping on cans before we hurl them into the recycling bin (maybe shouting things about our abusers as well).

What the counsellor and others might fear, I suppose, is that once the person has allowed themselves to think, 'I'm furious with my mother for the way she let the abuse continue,' or something like that, then the counsellor has a much harder job. And maybe she feels for her

172

client that now, with anger revealed and expressed, they might be more vulnerable and exposed – and maybe likely to go and have a disastrous bust-up row with their mother?

I can understand this theory (that any actual physical expression of anger could escalate to an outpouring of rage), and it makes sense that people might be afraid that this could get out of control. This gets us back to the crucial point that it is absolutely fine to feel anger and rage, but it is not right to go and bash someone.

When I ask Kate about it she points out that it can be very difficult for people to regulate their emotions. They can get switched on, but like a boiler without a thermostat, the emotion can get too intense and potentially explosive.

Physical expressions of anger must be controlled, not acted out on someone. I spent hours of my life as a teacher trying to teach that very basic concept to small children.

Keep yourself safe

In my view, can-jumping or cushion-killing is fine as long as you are aware that the anger will rise up within you as you stab or jump in fury (probably yelling all kinds of things I'd better not write here), and that feeling that anger can be scary.

So you need to set up some kind of safety net if you are going to explore your anger.

You must plan ways to keep yourself safe.

• Do the cushion-killing with a friend.

• Ask your self-help group to have a session on anger with lots of cans and cushions brought in to help the process.

• Talk it through with a therapist – if you have one.

The crucial thing is that you must keep safe. The rage could have been building up within you throughout your life, so it is risky to explore it.

How do we deal with our anger?

If you think that you are not angry, that's absolutely fine, but you could ask yourself if there are some bits of your life that could be outward expressions of anger in disguise – depression and physical illnesses such as tension headaches and so on.

I don't think there is any sense in which we *must* feel angry. If you don't feel it, that might mean you are beyond it, or that you aren't ready to deal with it yet.

I find it effective to think of some angry things I could do to people who I think have abused me. I know that some people would think that my fantasy wish to cut my step-father's penis off is as bad as actually doing it, but I don't think it is! I keep it as a funny idea.

I'm not at all suggesting that we rush off on some penis-lopping frenzy. We really mustn't harm someone because of our anger and rage. But it is funny to think about it. And that is a very effective way to break chains – to laugh and maybe also share the joke with a friend.

Various writers and psychologists have suggested that it is good for us to 'process' our rage – to find a way to make it less damaging by bringing it to the surface sufficiently to stop it being so poisonous inside us.

Processing our anger

Working with Ruth, Killer Whale and Wolf kept my anger manageable. I remember sitting with Ruth over many weeks twisting Suzie Penguin's flippers round and round as we talked and I denied my anger. I kept 'going out the window'. It wasn't until Ruth pointed out that Suzie Penguin was taking the worst of it onto her now curled-up flippers that I began to be a bit more honest.

I wrote at length in my journal about my feelings of being 'dead inside', as well as about the times when I could touch the anger – usually anger at someone else rather than my abusers.

This journal writing helped me enormously, both at the time and in reflecting on it months and years later.

Strategies for dealing with our anger and pent-up rage

1. Recognize that feeling *anything* is great. You've broken the chain of inner deadness and that's good.

2. When rage strikes, you can try deep 'belly' breathing. Put your hand just under your tummy button and when you breathe deeply your hand should move. Do a few deep breaths then exhale as much air as you can, imagining all the pent-up rage flowing out with your breath.

3. If someone says something and anger strikes, always count to five slowly before you react. That way you can consider a sensible and appropriate response.

4. BUT don't bottle it up. You will need to go to your journal to work out what is going on.

KEY POINTS

■ It's OK to be angry. It's a normal human emotion, but buried anger can turn into pent-up rage – and that can be problematic.

■ Anger is an emotion that always has some kind of hurt behind it, so we need to identify that hurt if we are to understand our anger.

■ Anger can involve a great deal of fear.

■ We can find safe and effective ways to find out more about our anger and rage so that we can break free of it.

■ It is common for survivors to be so angry they feel capable of hurting someone.

CHAIN BREAKING

1. Work on one or more of the strategies above. To help you to focus you might want to write yourself a note to stick by the kettle or on your mirror, for example, 'Why did I get so angry with Jake?'

2. Taking just one aspect of our anger at a time helps us to focus and makes it easier to find something out about ourselves. If we try to focus on anger in general, that is so vast that it could be too difficult to deal with. (That's probably why we do it! We all seem to avoid anything that involves actual change – and finding out about our anger is likely to change us.)

3. Try safe things like angry letters that you don't send. Even if writing isn't one of the things you like doing, writing these letters can be so healing – you let yourself touch the pain, let rip with the rage. No one is going to read it except you so you can say whatever you like. If your rage is with a family member who abused you, you can even go back to childhood (or adulthood) things they did to you. Be completely

honest – 'You wrecked my life' words can flow out of you.

Then it will feel much better (probably), so best to shred or burn the letter once your rage has settled – it wouldn't do for someone to find it and actually send it. Having said that though, I do tend to keep mine, often tucked into my journal where I find them months or years later. I find it helpful to skim read them, remember the deep feelings I had, then get rid of the letter so I don't ruminate on it for the next year.

4. Rather oddly we can feel anger in our body. I mentioned before my confusing deep hatred as a surge in my vagina. It isn't a turned-on kind of surge, it is furious pent-up rage and the deepest hatred you could ever imagine.

Try to notice if you feel anger in your body. Write it down so you can think about it. This could be a powerful way to 'uncover' and 'discover' your anger. When you feel anger, come back to this page. Try to write about the feelings of anger and also try to find the trigger that set you off.

'I think the trigger was…'

5. Can you get to the underlying hurts that are underneath your anger? (This has taken me years to work out, and I'm not at all sure I've got it all sussed even now. It must be one of those things that takes a lifetime.)

6. Look back at some of your writing about your own anger. Do you say things like, 'He made me angry…'?

We need to be careful not to blame others for making us angry. I've found this such a hard lesson to learn. We need to change from 'He made me angry' to 'I felt angry when…' We must take responsibility for our own feelings of anger. Nobody *makes* us angry. We choose to get angry – and that is OK. Angry feelings are normal. It's learning to express them (or contain them) safely that matters.

Remember
If you are going to try to uncover some of your rage you must keep yourself safe.

Every time you don't follow your inner guidance, you feel a loss of energy, loss of power, a sense of spiritual deadness.
SHAKTI GAWAIN

22 Healthy boundaries

Whatever kind of abuse we suffered it will have involved someone invading our personal space, and that can mean that we find it hard to keep sensible and safe boundaries around ourselves now.

This doesn't mean putting brick walls around ourselves and living in an impenetrable fortress (though that can seem inviting to some of us), but being balanced and open in relationships. Good boundaries are flexible. They let us choose with whom we are friendly and intimate. Developing good boundaries protects us from those people in our lives who are difficult to deal with or who are dysfunctional, or in some way trigger our memories.

What are boundaries?

Our inner life of thoughts, feelings, wants, intuitions, beliefs and feelings is at the core of our being, our True Self, or our Inner Child – some might call it our soul. This is who we are – the person we learn to understand – and eventually to appreciate. This is the sense we begin to develop as teenagers when we say, 'I'm starting to know who I am.' We need to know this True Self, to know who we are, before we can have healthy close relationships.

I have my personal space and it is different and quite separate from David's personal space, despite us having an intimate relationship. We are very 'close' to each other, but between us there is neutral space. I try not to invade his personal space just as he is good at not invading mine – even when it wobbles and shifts when I am 'triggered' or stressed by flashbacks and so on. I've had to learn to tell him when I can't cope with being near him.

With healthy boundaries we feel safe, complete, secure and loved. We know who we are and we are in touch with our inner life of wants, needs, feelings and so on.

> You shall be together even in the silent memory of God.
> But let there be spaces in your togetherness.
> And let the winds of the heavens dance between you.
> KAHLIL GIBRAN

Unhealthy boundaries

Abuse seems to switch us off in some weird way. We struggle to work out who we are as adolescents, and we can still be struggling with that well into adulthood.

I think this is like us repressing our memories. We also buried a sense of who we really are – that Self that we decided was bad and guilty.

Abuse diverts us away from who we truly are. We lose touch with our Inner Life, and obviously that is going to have far-reaching consequences. (Just to touch on the 'wallowing' thing again here – we're not 'wallowing', we're so out of touch we can't find who we really are.)

With unhealthy boundaries we can tend to:

• let people get inappropriately close, or keep them at an inappropriate distance and not dare trust anyone – so we can be single when we don't want that

• know so little about our Inner Child or True Self that we can be unable or unwilling to develop healthy boundaries and can therefore tend to let others mistreat us. We can tend to be abused all over again and not know how to stop it

• get upset easily (this is a big one for me)

• neglect our own needs and focus too much on the needs of others – this 'people pleasing' is partly what Americans call co-dependency

• be easily manipulated.

> *Submitting to others, rather than affirming our own reality, is the heart of co-dependence – we give up our own inner world in order to be accepted by others. Such co-dependence amounts to a self-betrayal. We give up ourselves in order to please, satisfy or impress others. By betraying our True Self, our sense of integrity and wholeness suffers. Our spirit wilts. Having healthy boundaries enables us to move from self-betrayal to self-affirmation, self-regard and self-trust.*
> JOHN AMODEO

How do I know if I have unhealthy boundaries?

There are many indicators of having unhealthy boundaries and I've picked out a few significant ones that I see in myself and in others. If you want to know more, the book by Charles Whitfield (see the resources section) is really good and so easy to read.

Here are some indicators of unhealthy boundaries:

1. BEING INDECISIVE

When David has a day off, he will sometimes say, 'What shall we do on Friday?' Quite often I will say, 'Oh, I don't know. You choose.' I recognize this indecision as me being a 'people pleaser', or it could be me genuinely wanting him to choose what he does on his day off. But I see in myself the tendency to be a bit too much of a people pleaser and not give my opinion enough, so that I can agree with people rather than have even a tiny bit of conflict.

But I'm much better than I was. (See – we do change!) I know my own mind a little better. I am more in touch with my inner wants and needs. But of course it is important that I don't go too far and just selfishly want to do what I want to do and not take into account the needs and wants of others.

2. BEING INAPPROPRIATELY DEMANDING OF OTHERS

Some survivors over-depend on others. Without having learned to develop our own healthy boundaries (perhaps because of the poor parenting we experienced as we grew up), we can find it hard to appreciate that everyone has limits and needs. Everyone wants their own space.

This can become a problem within survivors' friendships when, because of their very real needs, some survivors demand far too much of others. For example, sending an overwhelming number of text messages to another survivor who is already struggling with her own needs.

This kind of situation can lead to people feeling rejected, or other confusions that can arise in any relationships around those who are vulnerable.

3. BECOMING OVER-DEPENDENT

Linked with the point above, some survivors can come to over-depend on the professional and other support they are offered, leading to the sense that they would never be able to cope on their own. This loss of confidence and self-esteem can escalate to the point where a survivor becomes 'stuck'.

Perhaps this is similar to the ways in which prisoners can feel they would never cope if they were allowed out. We like our support structures around us and don't want things to change.

4. BEING OVER-SENSITIVE TO CRITICISM
Without appropriate boundaries, survivors can tend to take criticism so personally that it can ruin relationships. For example, if an over-dependent survivor has the dependence pointed out, he or she could retreat into that common conviction that it just proves that the world would be a better place if they were dead.

With no firm boundaries, their fragile existence is shattered.

5. BEING CONFUSED ABOUT ANGER
Without healthy boundaries, anger can be seen as so terrifying that it must be avoided at all costs. Or the anger may be acted out in violence, perhaps with a lack of understanding of the boundaries that others have and need.

6. FEELING A SENSE OF SHAME AND GUILT
Sometimes, when some small thing goes wrong, just about every survivor I know retreats very quickly into 'it was all my fault'. Again this is about our fragile self-esteem. Some of us can only see ourselves as wicked and guilty. We are ashamed that we exist.

7. SPENDING INAPPROPRIATE AMOUNTS OF TIME CARING FOR OTHERS
Of course it is good to care for others, but if it goes too far we can be left with too little time to care for ourselves adequately. We can get kicks from needing to be needed in an over-the-top way.

8. AVOIDING TIME ALONE.
We all need time alone to think. If we don't take 'time out' to reflect on our lives, to write or draw, to re-create, we are ignoring that huge inner part of ourselves that needs nurturing – our Inner Child.

9. GETTING INTO AND STAYING IN UNHEALTHY RELATIONSHIPS
It's amazing how abused people seem to get involved with abusers. The child of the alcoholic parents gets involved with the alcoholic

partner – this is the co-dependency again. We all need to look carefully at our relationships. If they are unhealthy we need to get out of them or change them, though the latter is very hard to do. But we can learn to be more assertive – without being abusive or aggressive – and put forward our wants and needs in an open way, ready to respond to the needs and wants of the other person. (Or escape to a safe place if the conversation isn't going very well!)

10. FEELING RESPONSIBLE FOR OTHER PEOPLE'S FEELINGS
If we feel overly responsible for others we can again be avoiding our own Inner Self. Everyone is responsible for their own feelings, but our struggle to free ourselves from our chains somehow gets in the way of being rational about this. We do the guilt and shame again – 'It's all my fault they feel that bad.' We might even go out of our way to please the person so that they will like us. This links to the next point.

11. GOING OVER THE TOP IN DOING THINGS FOR PEOPLE
I find this in myself. I'm so anxious for people to like me and approve of me that I do too much to gain their favour. I find it really hard not to do that because I can't split it off from appropriate generosity.

Repairing and building boundaries
Charles Whitfield gives an outline of the process for healing our True Self. He says that to heal my True Self:

I need to go within, into my inner life. Over time I...
- *Identify and grieve my ungrieved hurts, losses and traumas*
- *Get my healthy human needs met*
- *Work through my 'core' recovery issues.'*

CHARLES WHITFIELD

This outline of the healing process is very close to the process of 'uncovery', 'discovery' and 'recovery' that many psychologists use.

Our healing begins with us identifying the awful ways in which we were mistreated in childhood. Some people find that so horrendous that they have no early memories at all, so the first stage is to find at least some detail within our buried memories, then to grieve for what we have lost.

181

That grieving is crucial. Just as we build up inner stress if we don't grieve when someone we love dies, so we build up stress and confusion if we don't grieve for our own losses, for example loss of being safe, or loss of emotional security if incest is an issue in our home.

Depression is almost always about some kind of loss. Abuse is the same – we lose something significant.

I lost the whole of my childhood. I remember nothing before going to High School at eleven, but now I'm beginning to get memories back – memories of brutal beatings.

A WOMAN SURVIVOR AGED 30, WHO WAS SUFFERING FROM POST-NATAL DEPRESSION

Charles Whitfield identifies the next stage of repairing our boundaries as getting our human needs met. We need love, security, a safe place to be, a sense that we belong somewhere and so on. We need these basic needs as we try to 'discover' more about our Inner Self – our soul.

Working through 'core issues'

What Whitfield means by 'core issues' is any issue that keeps impeding our recovery. Trust is one example that many survivors find hard. If we refuse to trust we can feel chained up in a pit of loneliness – but learning to trust can take us years, so it is a core issue that we need to work through.

Other core issues are mentioned throughout this book and include:

• struggling with low self-esteem (our lack of belief in ourselves keeps us very securely held down with chains and often in deep depression as well)

• our fear of being abandoned – this is a huge one for me

• confusion over how to be 'real': Who am I? What is at the core of my being? What is my True Self?

• overwhelming feelings that we find hard to control: extreme fear, our sense of worthlessness, our guilt and our sense of shame – 'I don't deserve a good life'

• difficulties with anger and conflict

• difficulties understanding our real feelings

182

- feeling inappropriately responsible for others

- problems with control – needing to control others too much or finding it hard to control ourselves

- giving and receiving love.

Strategies for dealing with our 'core issues'

I've dealt with ways we work through and heal our 'core issues' throughout this book, sometimes in lists of strategies or in chain breaking activities.

Here is a list of strategies for healing our 'core issues'. I've partly based it on those Charles Whitfield suggests throughout his book:

1. I'm really pleased that Charles sees writing as a powerful tool for recovery. It can be hugely important in our recovery as a record of feelings and ideas that are there in front of us, and we can come back to them and reflect on them.

2. Reflection is very powerful. Research evidence shows that reflection is a powerful aspect of human growth and personal and social development:

❖ We discover our inner life through reflection.

❖ We change by reflecting.

❖ We break chains by reflecting.

So don't always rush on to the next thing. Stop. Think. Meditate. Pray. Spend at least ten minutes with one of your creatures or holding something you treasure. I need Eric when I reflect, or Suzie-doll and Shadow if I am confused.

3. Talk with safe people – being specific about the problem that you are trying to work through. If you aren't fortunate enough to have a therapist, go to a self-help group or join an on-line one.

4. Write and/or talk a bit more about that specific issue.

5. Set yourself a specific task about your specific issue such as, 'What can I learn from this issue?' Write it down or you will forget.

6. Reflect a bit more.

7. Repeat the process as often as you need to, then let go if you can. When we've worked on our specific issue, we may take weeks or months or years to sort an issue out. It's good to find a way of letting go because this is important for our inner healing.

KEY POINTS

■ Because our personal space was invaded by abusers, one outcome is that we will tend to have issues about boundaries.

■ We need healthy boundaries to function well as human beings.

■ We improve our boundaries by working though our difficult issues such as anger or fear of being abandoned.

CHAIN BREAKING

1. Look at the list above of seven suggestions for dealing with one of our 'core' issues.

2. Choose something that is bothering you, or something you want to work through – I'm trying to deal with my 'people pleasing'. You might be trying to deal with facing conflict, or dealing with a relationship that has just broken down; or you might be learning to trust someone who seems to care about you – but you are frightened of commitment.

3. When you have identified just one thing, start by writing about it and work your way down the list of suggestions. Any order is fine – there is no set rule.

4. Over the next few days, weeks and months, try to work more on this one issue.

5. If you can 'let go' at the end that's fantastic, but you are not a failure if you find your worries and concerns coming back when you thought you had 'let go'. Remember the healing helix. We come back to the same things over and over again as we heal. That's 'normal'.

6. Assertiveness training courses are sometimes run at adult education colleges and learning to be more assertive can help us in many ways, including getting out of unhealthy relationships.

Remember
It wasn't your fault that your boundaries were invaded.

Snipers are people who undermine your efforts to break unhealthy relationship patterns.
JODY HAYES

23 Forgive and forget?

If there is one issue guaranteed to get survivors going it is forgiveness. Someone uses that 'f' word and there is a sharp intake of breath, probably because so many of us have had some pressure to 'forgive and forget' *now*. I think that mostly that advice is inappropriate – not least because it is silly to link forgetting with forgiving. I would think it is impossible to forget about abuse once you've recovered your memory.

I've sat in discussions about forgiveness with people who have been abused. We've emailed each other, cried, wondered, become confused and at times given up because it all seems too hard – too complicated.

So I set about reading as many books about it as I could, from the South African Truth and Reconciliation thoughts to earnest treaties in which we are all promised total healing if only we could completely forgive *now*.

What forgiveness isn't

There is a lorry load of misconceptions out there about forgiveness and I've already mentioned the linking of forgiving with forgetting.

No one would expect the rape victims Jill Saward or Alice Seebold to *forget* their horrific rapes (see references to their books in the resources at the back). They are unlikely to forget, but they might 'let go' to find release from their pain.

I don't know where this hopelessly misguided 'forgive and forget' idea came from, but it underpins the British culture that I live in – and I believe it to be a dangerous belief that is seriously screwing up the lives of anyone who has experienced any 'big' hurt.

Maybe this 'forgetting' that people want us to do is so that we will stop talking about the abuse. If they could only get us to forget it, they then wouldn't need to engage with the thought that we are in pain. Would us forgetting maybe make it easier for people?

It isn't an event

One thing that confuses our thoughts on forgiveness is to think of it as an event: 'I forgave her at 5pm on Tuesday'. I really don't think this is how it works.

Yes, we have times when our thoughts change. I've had times when

I have realized I have started to forgive someone. With my mother, I realized long ago that I had forgiven her, but I discovered that forgiveness is more of a process than a 'one off' event.

I see the forgiving process as another helix, just like the healing helix on page 158. We need to keep coming back to the same things over and over again.

Turn the other cheek

Another fundamental misconception about forgiveness arises from the teaching of Jesus. I'm told by a variety of friends of different faiths that Jesus is seen as the greatest example of a forgiving person.

Yes, that makes sense, but I still think there are some misconceptions rattling around in all of that.

Take Jesus' teaching about 'turning the other cheek' – most people I've come across interpret that as not retaliating. Yes, that's a good way to live our lives – hitting back is the way to start a war, not usually the way to live in peace.

BUT, if we take our non-retaliating to an extreme, we can end up with a nauseating why-don't-you-just-walk-all-over-me attitude. That, I think, is wrong because that would mean that we might not be standing up for justice.

Where is the justice?

Justice is terribly important, and it has got lost to some extent in the culture I live in, especially within the world of Christian survivors. We are told to forgive. We ask, 'Where is justice?'

People who suffer domestic violence are often encouraged to forgive and forget and stay with their partner, but often without any help to address the violence from that partner. This keeps forgiveness as something that the victim must do rather than a situation that needs action from the abuser. This is incredibly irritating from the point of view of adults who are being abused, because all the time they are being told they must 'forgive and move on' without there being even one jot of justice – and sometimes nothing at all being done about their personal safety. (Sometimes in domestic violence situations this can result in their murder.)

Don't forgive too soon

Don't Forgive Too Soon is the title of a really good book I've come across.

Wow! What a message within a title. I just had to read the book.

The most significant thing that the authors of the book explore is a different understanding of some Christian thinking such as 'turning the other cheek'.

Most people, whatever their faith – or if they have no faith – believe that Christians are told never to retaliate (even in words) and that if someone hits us, we're commanded to allow the attacker to hit us again, and forgive instantly. This, the authors of the book say, is a complete misunderstanding of this part of the Bible.

The authors (some of the Linn family) have explored the thinking of Walter Wink, a Christian who has gone back to the teachings of Jesus and put these into the cultural context of the first century. The outcome is that we end up with quite a different slant (and one that appeals to me and makes any understanding of forgiveness much more realistic) on the teaching of Jesus surrounding ideas of retaliation, justice and forgiveness.

The new thinking goes something like this:

The Romans were in charge of Palestine at the time, so when Jesus said, 'Turn the other cheek,' he would have been talking to an audience of ordinary people within that context, illustrating his stories with aspects of the Roman and Palestinian culture of that time.

What Jesus actually said didn't mean you to abandon justice and allow the person to hit you again. He would be talking about this kind of incident that could happen between an ordinary Palestinian and a Roman soldier.

Let's suppose an ordinary Palestinian farmer accidentally got in the way of a Roman soldier and ended up being hit. The soldier would strike the farmer using the back of his right hand, on the farmer's right cheek – that apparently was the way to hit someone 'beneath' you. The backhanded slap would be a sign of contempt.

To turn the other cheek the farmer would turn his head, indicating to the soldier to hit him on his other cheek. But to do that, the soldier would (using his right hand) have to hit with his open right hand on the farmer's left cheek. The soldier would probably not want to do that because to hit someone in that way was to acknowledge that they were your equal. No way would a Roman soldier want to make a Palestinian an equal.

So in telling us to offer our other cheek, Jesus was meaning not 'OK just hit me again, never mind about justice, go ahead and walk all over me' (an alarmingly common interpretation of what some say Jesus meant). Instead, Walter Wink and the Linns say that offering your other cheek in this way is like saying, 'Give me the status I deserve – I'm not beneath you.'

Now that is a revolution in understanding Western Christian culture! The assumption so many make, that we are expected to forgive at all costs by turning the other cheek, often ignoring justice, is a complete misunderstanding of that aspect of the teaching of Jesus.

Carla's story

Let me tell you Carla's story of what happened when she went to an Easter service at a church. She tells of an enthusiastic young male vicar who gives a sermon about the horrors Jesus went through during his crucifixion.

The vicar points to Jesus being stripped naked and beaten. 'Have you ever been stripped naked and beaten?' he says.

'Well, yes,' says Carla to herself. (Her experience of childhood abuse was brutal.)

'Have you ever been whipped and made to keep going when you are exhausted?' the young vicar goes on.

'Well, yes,' says Carla to herself.

'Have you been injured and taunted – made to suffer so that your life was in danger?'

'Well, yes,' says Carla to herself.

As Carla tells the story, her face is creased with grief and there are tears forming in her eyes.

'Then he ended the sermon,' she says, 'by saying that because Jesus went through all of that with no complaint, so all of us must just take what comes to us in life, silently. We have to suffer like Jesus.'

Carla cannot help her tears. 'So you see, that vicar just took away any thoughts of a person standing up to domestic violence. He seems to be teaching that every child who is abused at home needs just to put up with it. Does Jesus really teach that I turn my back on that child and tell him to put up with it?'

Carla has hit on a crucial misunderstanding both of the teaching of Jesus and of forgiveness.

It cannot be right for us to be expected just to sit back and take abuse!

We all need to stand up for justice.

I believe Jesus was doing a 'one off' thing when he went willingly to the cross, just as Aslan let the White Witch kill him in *The Lion the Witch and the Wardrobe*. Death can have a sacrificial meaning. As Aslan put it:

> '...when a willing victim who had committed no treachery was killed in a traitor's stead... Death itself would start working backwards.'
> C.S. LEWIS

Carla never went to that church again!

Jesus on the cross

Another mega misconception that underpins unrealistic views about forgiveness is to do with Jesus on the cross.

I hear people saying that Jesus forgave his abusers when he was on the cross. He is even quoted as saying, 'Father, I forgive them because they don't know what they are doing.'

Yes, Jesus says to his Father that the stupid people don't know what they are doing – and as I've said, Jesus gave up his life as a willing victim. His plan all along was to let them kill him. But it must have been hell.

What he actually says is, '*Father* forgive them.'

This is maybe the most important sentence in the whole book if you are a Christian and you are suffering from people around you doing the you-must-forgive-instantly stuff.

Consider this:

• What Jesus said was 'Father, forgive them.'

• Maybe his next line was, '...because I can't just at the moment, nails through my hands and feet, spear in my side, my mum weeping and all that – so, Father, could you please do the forgiving for me?'

OK, I invented that sentence, but the fact is that Jesus did not say from the cross that he forgave his abusers. He showed us that ultimately it is God who does the forgiving.

However, what is true about the life of Jesus is that he was a forgiving kind of person and in his teachings we find many exhortations for us to forgive those who hurt us. The trouble is that this has somehow metamorphosed into the glib 'instant forgiveness' teaching that has crept into our culture and that has cruelly and horribly messed up the lives of many survivors with burdens of guilt.

Forgiving is an attitude

If we can get our thinking away from forgiveness being something we might do next Saturday, we move towards a different way of thinking.

Forgiveness is:

• an attitude

• a process that takes time

• about relationships and the community we live in

• about how we treat those around us in our ordinary everyday lives – we 'live' forgiveness.

Some people are loving, honest and caring. Others are selfish and hit out at people as a first reaction – probably we've all come across people like that. They don't have a forgiving attitude.

Grandma and the pennies

I think that this forgiving attitude in the ordinary everyday things is like the way my grandmother talked about money. She would say, 'Take care of the pennies (small amounts of money) and the pounds (large amounts of money) will look after themselves.'

If we cultivate in ourselves a loving and caring attitude to those around us, then the 'big' things like letting go and forgiving our abuser/s will come in their own time.

The Lord's Prayer

Some Christian survivors have a serious problem with saying, 'Forgive us our sins as we forgive those who sin against us' in the Lord's Prayer. They feel that means 'forgive instantly or God won't forgive you'.

That's another major misconception. This 'tit for tat' mechanical forgiving doesn't at all reflect the fact that God loves us all unconditionally (though some people choose not to accept that love). If you are a Christian and you don't believe in that unconditional love, you have some work to do on that. (You could read Philip Yancey's book, *What's So Amazing about Grace?*)

I believe God loves us. Full stop.

God loves us whether we are in a furious rage with our abusers, or hung up on the thoughts of taking them to court, or so utterly depressed about the whole thing that we feel suicidal, or in any other state of mind you think some people might not approve of.

Our Great Creator who made blue butterflies and polar bear cubs goes on loving us whatever.

If we go back to the point that forgiveness is an attitude and is about relationships rather than something we might do tomorrow, we can see that the Lord's Prayer is not saying we must do the instant quick fix forgiveness now. It is saying that we need to live a life in which we love and care, have a forgiving attitude, and strive for justice and peace.

We can do all those loving things *and still be really angry with our abusers* and feel that it is so difficult to forgive them that we wonder if we ever will.

That is OK.

Those of us who avoid church because of scary things like saying the Lord's Prayer are being misled. '…as we forgive those who sin against us' needs to be balanced with what I call The Millstone Factor and with the whole concept of time and forgiveness.

The Millstone Factor

I was taught at junior school about the things that Jesus said and I've always liked that bit where he says that if anyone hurts a little child, it would be better for them if they had a millstone (these are very heavy) strung round their neck and were chucked into a pond.

That means they die.

Here it is, straight from the most forgiving person the world has ever seen, 'You abuse one of my little ones and that's it mate. You're dead.'

What some people don't allow for when they do the you-must-forgive-now-or-you-go-to-hell stuff is that abuse is traumatic – and therefore difficult to forgive.

Take my supermarket trolley thoughts. If you accidentally hurt me with your trolley as I'm trying to reach for the tinned tomatoes, and you say 'Sorry', I will almost certainly say, 'That's OK.' Even if it hurts me, I will immediately release you if you didn't mean to do it. However, if you ram me deliberately and I can see in your face you meant to hurt me, and you say 'Sorry' with a grin on your face, I'm not going to say, 'That's OK.' I'm much more likely to be angry and glare at you – but hopefully will not retaliate by hurling tins of tomatoes at you.

If there is no sincere apology, I don't have to forgive you right there and then. I can stay with my rage for a bit and feel quite hurt that you would do that to me. In my own time I will let it all go for my own sake

– so that I'm not still hanging on to hateful thoughts and risking becoming 'bitter and twisted'.

If, however, you run me down with your trolley late one night in the car park and sexually assault me – the police find you but you deny doing it, you look me right in the face, daring me to take you to court – what then do we make of '…as we forgive those who sin against us'?

Not a quick 'I forgive you', that's for sure! I'd need time. I'd need lots of hugs.

Yes, I'd know that long term I will 'let go for my own mental health' (we keep coming back to that – it's my most crucial chain breaking equipment), but I'm not likely to do any of that instant forgiving that so many people seem to believe is right.

Superficial forgiveness is only likely to build up more stress and confusion within us, and those who push us to 'forgive and forget' are actually getting close to abusing us all over again.

There are things to be worked through if our 'letting go' is to be meaningful and if we are to come through the trauma as a healed and happy person.

Time and forgiving
Much of the confusion about forgiving seems to me to be about time, so let's think through some scenarios.

If someone, male or female, is brutally raped and left for dead, as they see their attackers run off down the lane, is their first thought likely to be, 'I forgive them'?

Probably not.

The person is much more likely to think, 'I must get help. Where is my phone? Please God, help me. Do I dare involve the police or shall I just try to crawl home and get a shower?'

How much does it matter if they get to the sentence 'I forgive those rapists' in ten minutes, ten days, ten weeks, ten months, ten years, or if they take decades – or even die before they can say those words?

I don't think it matters one tiny minuscule bit.

There can't be some kind of universal time limit on forgiving, or even on 'letting go for our own mental health'.

Trauma takes time to work through and it hurts to admit that inside we are a tangled-up holocaust of hate and anger. But if we deny the depth of our hurt, all we do is make our recovery slower.

God's work?

I read a survivor's story of her struggle with forgiving the people who abused her and she tells how in her struggle a wise woman said to her, 'It is not for you to forgive. That is God's work.' The writer tells how from then on she experienced freedom from that terrible burden that so many of us carry, the awful responsibility of forgiving.

It is God's work to do the forgiving!

Of course we still have to work out our relationships and so on with those who abused us, but we can hand the whole lot over to God.

I thought this a brilliant strategy!

This is roughly what I've said to God:

'Here you are. I can't cope with this forgiving stuff. I don't know how to do it. But I don't want to end up some bitter old resentful person who is horrible to be with. I want to be free.

'So here you are – all of my struggle, all of my fears that you might reject me, all of my rage – I can't seem to get the idea of forgiveness inside me and understand it. It is all here for you. It is no longer my burden.

'Thank you.'

Strategies for exploring forgiveness

1. Try the strategy above. It works for me.

2. Try to put aside all the sense of being pushed into forgiving. No one has the right to judge anyone else. You 'let go' in your own way and time.

3. Try to identify some easier bits of 'letting go' in your circumstances. For example, if you still see your abuser/s, or those who know of your accusations, you could try not to keep going on about the abuse. Your sister might want to do the washing up with you without you raising all the painful issues. If you do need to talk about it, ask for an hour to talk things through.

Just shutting up about it all can be the start of us 'letting go'.

Stages of forgiving

One of the things that can help us in the difficult process of forgiving is to consider what the authors of the book *Don't Forgive Too Soon* suggest. They say there are five stages in the forgiving process, and a useful strategy for helping us to 'let go' is to consider which of these stages we are in at the moment.

The stages are:

1. Denial. Of course we don't want to face what is happening.

2. Anger. Of course we are angry – that anger is the power and incentive we need to find creative ways to forgive and move on.

3. Bargaining. Of course we go into bargaining. 'You must apologize first.' Absolutely right – no apology and we are heading for a long process of trying to 'let go'. In the film *Something about Amelia*, she gets an apology, a total admission of guilt. 'It was my fault. You are not to blame in any way. What I did was wrong.'

Most abused people don't get that. In fact they usually get vehement denial – and if there is one thing that is going to scupper the whole idea of us 'letting go' it is that total denial from our abuser/s. 'I did nothing wrong. I never touched you. You made it all up, you evil little minx.' (Or even worse, 'I did it because I love you.')

4. Grief. Of course we feel grief. We lost our childhood. We lost our innocence. We lost the ability to trust. We were faced with such violence and such brutality that we couldn't make sense of it, and our world was rocked for ever.

The adult victim loses too – a sense of safety, a sense that life can be good, and their sense that they are worthwhile people.

5. Acceptance. Maybe we don't all get as far as this final stage of acceptance – and that's OK. In the earlier stages we might have said, 'I want to let go for the sake of my own mental health,' but now we might be able to sense a deeper forgiveness.

Remember though that these stages could give the impression that the forgiveness process is neat and tidy and predictable, which it isn't at all. We are liable to keep looping around, re-visiting things again and again just as in the healing helix on page 158. For example, we might find our anger welling up when we thought we had left it behind and so on.

Healthy forgiving
Healthy forgiveness is about first working through the most basic inner

parts of our soul that have become wounded through the abuse. The five stages above would be part of our 'uncovery' and 'discovery'.

- Healthy forgiveness takes time.

- Anger, rage, grief, spacing out because it is all too overwhelming – all of that is part of the forgiving process.

- The shouts of 'I'm never going to forgive them' are all part of the anger.

- To be angry is to be on the way to forgiving.

- To feel blank is on the way to being angry, so blank, spaced-out feelings too are part of forgiving.

If you are reading this book looking for help and healing, you are almost certainly wanting to 'let go for your own mental health', and that is quite a long way through the process of forgiving.

So you are already into some forgiving chain breaking!

KEY POINTS

■ Forgiving takes time. It is not a one-off event.

■ Forgiving is difficult.

■ Forgiving can start with our intention gradually to 'let go' and our decision to move forward into something much more creative.

■ 'Letting go' need not be related in any way to our abusers apologizing.

■ It's God who does the forgiving!

CHAIN BREAKING

1. Identify which of the five stages (on page 195) you are in at the moment. (You might be lurching around more than one stage.)

2. Part of learning to 'let go' is a bit like turning around our negative thinking.

This is a really big area for me, the ruminator – it's all too easy to go back into the murky mess of childhood or think about my tyrannical boss. If I let my mind replay bad situations, my heart beats faster and I can end up feeling anxious and stressed.

I must make a conscious decision to 'let go' and replace these old thoughts with more positive mental images.

I tell myself:

❖ You are no longer a victim, you're a survivor.

❖ This is old stuff. You'll feel happier if you think about the siskins on the bird feeder instead.

❖ Move on! Don't behave as if you were still chained up in all that junk.

> *Fill your minds with everything that is true, everything that is noble, everything that is good and pure, everything that we love and honour, and everything that can be thought virtuous or worthy of praise.*
> THE APOSTLE PAUL WRITING TO THE PEOPLE IN PHILIPPI

3. Can you write/draw your own 'list' of more positive mental images you will use to replace the old ones? (Things you really like such as the feel of the waves as you surf towards the beach.)

4. Suzie Penguin helps me to forgive. Her cuddly softness cannot contemplate the harshness of clinging on to resentment. I want to be soft and gentle too – I want to have a forgiving attitude. Look among your special things. What could remind you to let go? What about a fossil? Mine remind me not to get crushed to death in the rock.

5. Although revenge is not a good idea, I think *not* taking revenge is an early stage of 'letting go'. In your journal, list some things that 'letting go' is, such as:

❖ not actively destroying the life of our abuser

❖ not sending hate mail and ringing them up and doing heavy breathing to freak them out

❖ not wishing upon them terrible things such as a long, slow, lingering and painful death. (I took a long time to move beyond that with my tyrannical boss!)

There are probably many more 'not' things you can imagine and add to your list.

6. Now list some practical things that 'letting go' is, such as:

❖ sending a birthday and Christmas card

❖ wishing things could resolve (after they have apologized)

❖ deciding that you are not going to let the abuser wreck your life, so you are choosing for your own health to 'let go'.

What my list does for me is help me to see that I am at least on the road towards 'letting go'. I'm in the process of forgiving.

Remember
We can make a deliberate decision to change our chained-up awful life into the best life anyone could have. Be bold and aim high!

Crucially what we are doing by 'letting go' is empowering ourselves – we are taking back control of our lives and not allowing our abuser/s have one jot of influence over our lives now.

> *All our study of psychology and our experience in counseling told us that it's unhealthy to passively suffer abuse... Jesus invites us to a forgiveness that, far from being passive and self-abusive, actively resists evil, maintains our dignity and invites the person who hurt us to recall his or her own dignity.*
> DENNIS, SHEILA AND MATTHEW LINN

24 Struggling with forgiving

Forgiving is hard. It makes juggling with chainsaws look easy. But as we saw in the last chapter, forgiving isn't just that final stage (that we might never reach) of knowing we have forgiven completely. Forgiving starts with tears, anger, 'If only…', more tears and more rage – and our growing ability to 'let go', even if that is just to prevent ourselves plummeting into a totally chained-up pit of resentment.

Even 'letting go' can be hard and I totally understand people I know who are determined that they must have justice, or that they must have an apology before they will forgive. Some of the stories I've heard from abused people are utterly horrific.

One young man, Aiden, was telling me about how angry he gets when people tell him he must forgive, or God will not forgive him any of the things he does wrong. He told me how the pastor at his church had reprimanded him (again), saying Aiden should forgive his abuser (an older brother, Carl):

> I told him, that if my brother would say sorry it might be different. But Carl even denies it all. I told my pastor that when he has had a penis rammed into his backside day after day from the age of three until the age of twelve, when he has been threatened with all kinds of knives, warned that his mother would never believe him and send him into a home, been bullied and beaten so often by a brother twelve years older than him, then, and then only, I will listen to words from the pastor about forgiveness.
>
> AIDEN AGED 28

Healing trauma
Aiden has a point.

And it's not for any of us to look at someone who is finding forgiving very difficult and to think that we know the answer to their life's problems. Yes, we can encourage others to 'let go'. We can talk of the risk of us becoming embittered. But let's look back to those stages Judith Herman identifies in recovering from trauma that we looked at in chapter three.

- Establishing safety

- Reconstructing the traumatic events so that they make some kind of sense.

- Restoring the connections between survivors and their community.

All these come before forgiving, so the question 'Have you forgiven him?' might get the answer 'Yes', but equally it might get the very good honest answer:

'I'm in the process of doing that as I recover from the trauma of abuse.'

What's bad about forgiveness?

So far I've implied that forgiveness is a good, though difficult, thing – an attitude of mind in which we are in healthy relationships with those around us. (Remember that a healthy relationship with any of your abusers could mean you don't go within a mile of them.)

I've said that the forgiving process can be long and take years, but I've been clearly on the side of 'letting go for our own mental health'.

I've said that the instant kind of forgiveness and the 'forgive and forget' mentality are dire and are to be avoided. But there can be other aspects of forgiving that some think of as bad.

> I will... continue my attempt to offer objections to forgiveness and to counsel cautions with respect to its hasty adoption as a response to wrongdoing. In my view such a response risks compromising some very important values – for example, self-respect.
> JEFFRIE G. MURPHY

Self-respect is so very hard to hang on to after we have been abused, when our internal voice is saying, 'I'm such a hopeless and worthless person and it was all my fault.' So for some survivors, to be told they *must* forgive, well before they are anywhere near ready to do so, can mean that they need to let go of the very little self-respect they have managed to keep hold of.

Some people feel they would have to deny who they are, or do something dishonest, if they were to forgive their abusers. They cannot bear to suffer any more 'loss of face'. This is a very difficult problem to get over because it involves who we are – our Inner Self – and we may have lost so much after the violation of abuse that we cannot contemplate losing our Inner Self as well.

I'll never forgive them

We hear this bold statement often. So are some people saying that some things are so evil that it wouldn't be right to forgive them?

Some Jewish people say they won't forgive the holocaust.

'I'll never forgive them' is scrawled as graffiti on the walls in the Palestinian Jenine refugee camp in reaction to the modern state of Israel.

I heard a young man say 'I'll never forgive them' last night on BBC television. He was removed from his home and family in response to social workers believing that children on his estate in the north of England were being subjected to satanic sexual abuse.

The abuse was never proved. The parents were found innocent, and a decade on, those children grieve for that part of their childhood that was taken away because of errors of judgment by adults.

The taped interviews with the children were horrific. Little children pleaded to go home to mummy. But instead they were grilled by adults about sex – and the children were clearly suffering.

Trying to hang on to some of their self-respect, some survivors find that they cannot forgive without giving up some of who they are. Trying to cling on to their Inner Self, maybe for some all they can say is, 'I'll never forgive them'. Or it might be that some feel that to forgive would be to condone what was done – especially when an abuser is never brought to justice (the majority of cases). And I still see this 'I'll never forgive' attitude as part of the forgiving process. It is the anger showing – and that is good and to be expected.

It would be quite different if she would admit she did it but she just says she did nothing. So why should I forgive her if she won't say sorry? If she did apologize I might be able to forgive her.
BRIAN AGED 28, WHO WAS ABUSED BY HIS MOTHER SEXUALLY, EMOTIONALLY AND PHYSICALLY.

Make the first move?

Another 'bad' idea in some books about forgiveness is the thought that most problems are not one-sided – almost inevitably the person who feels innocent has done something to make things go wrong. So the theory goes that we, who feel innocent, need to make the first move towards the person who we feel wronged us.

Although I'm in favour of this view in theory, I don't think it is appropriate in cases of abuse, such as child abuse, any abuse of power and so on. (It's a bit hard to think of any instances of abuse where it would be appropriate for the survivor to go first and apologize, but it is possible that some instances might exist. A few women have said to me that they wondered if they played a part in some sexual abuse when they were adults.)

But the idea that survivors must make the first move and apologize to their abusers must be totally wrong.

I can see how we might make a move that might help the abusers to apologize, such as keeping family contacts going, giving them the opportunity to say sorry. But on the whole, survivors apologizing first is not only inappropriate, but dangerous in that survivors already have more guilt than they need. They need to dump that guilt, not let it grow even more by being told to make the first move!

How do we know when we have forgiven?
When I try to 'let go' I always wonder what it feels like to forgive. Am I supposed to feel something special?

Take my mother. She is dead now and when I think of that I'm filled with relief. That's a feeling, so I know I'm feeling something.

I think I've forgiven her everything, but I don't feel syrupy sweet things about her. My perception of her was that she was a manipulative, cruel, selfish abuser.

Forgiving her hasn't made me like her. I feel more sorry for her as the years go by. I think she probably did the parenting thing as best she could, but it really wasn't very good – possibly because she stayed so wrapped up in her own difficulties.

So I think if we 'let go', we can still think the truth about our abusers.

Forgiveness is part of the love that casts out fear and part of the truth that sets free.
DAVID ATKINSON

Wishing them well?
Years ago I was in a discussion about what forgiveness is. The leader

took as our starting point that forgiveness is 'when you start to wish the abuser well'.

But I didn't feel at all as if I was wishing my abusers well – except for my mother. I was still feeling blank about Ernie, my step-father.

But I began to see that I had long ago forgiven my older brother in that I never refer to his abuse; I really care about him; I hope he is happy. Because he hardly ever communicates with me (mostly a grunt is about his limit but there are occasional sentences) it is hard to know if he is happy or not, but I do what I can to stay calm and friendly even when he goes into his one track record of 'How can you be a writer? You can't even spell.'

Despite this, I wish him well.

But my uncle is quite different. He was my only adult male blood relative. He could have significantly contributed positive things to my life. Do I wish him well? No (partly because he is dead). I would never have had the courage to talk to him about it in the hope of getting an apology. He probably thought fondling the boobs of a teenage niece was quite an acceptable thing to do. (Times have changed, thank goodness, and pinching bottoms and so on is now seen for what it is, sexual harassment.)

Wow, I really am 'in touch with my feelings' about my uncle! Writing this, I'm in a rage. My hands are trembling. I realize I am grinding my teeth and feeling tense. (I'll take this as a positive thing because I'm not that great at feeling anger, and I'm not that great at 'being in touch' with my feelings.)

Allowing ourselves time

When I came to edit this chapter, to my delight I found that I really did have some feelings of having forgiven my uncle! I've changed! (We do change – let's hang on to that idea.)

But I'm not sure I've even started to forgive my step-father. So I suspect I might still have some unresolved thinking about him chained down inside me and I'm trying to find a way forward from that.

At times I can almost feel forgiving towards him. I'm pretty sure his father – who also abused me – could possibly have abused my step-father as a child. And at times my step-father was kindly towards me. So I suppose I might be setting out on the forgiving journey with him in that I want to 'let it all go'. I don't want him to have a hold over me still.

But one of the strange things about my relationship with my step-father (he has been dead for thirty years) is that I still feel very little anger towards him. I just feel numb. I don't even want to think about it. I feel in some weird way that he is still capable of sending rage and violence in my direction!

When I talked about this with Ruth, she said that I am carrying inside me the image of this terrifying step-father, which is what the child part of me understands and knows about at gut level. Children aren't reasonable, so this terrifying image has almost nothing to do with reality, logic or reasonableness.

So I wonder if I will feel the rage for him first before I can forgive? Do I *need* to *feel* that rage before I can forgive? I don't know.

Maybe the little child can't forgive?

One important thought about the loss of face problem is that the adult 'us' might well eventually be able to 'let go' – even move right along to being able to forgive completely – but what about that hurt little child within us? (Even for adult victims, their Inner Child is deeply bruised and invaded during abuse.)

Maybe what is causing us so much trouble as we struggle to let go enough to feel free of our abuser's power, is that we can let go in our head. We know it makes sense. But our Inner Child cannot yet forgive – or even let go.

And that is OK.

In terms of the stages of forgiveness and our attempts to 'let go', maybe our Inner Child is struggling along behind our Adult Self – three or four turns of the forgiving helix behind us – still numb and unable to work out what a forgiving attitude is anyway.

Forgiving ourselves

Most survivors have problems with forgiving themselves. Surprisingly, the thought of forgiving ourselves seems to be a new one to many.

I know I can never forgive myself.
A SURVIVOR

At the back of this inability to forgive and love ourselves hangs those ever-present five survivor words.

It was all my fault.

This is what we say. I do even now, when I feel free of many of my chains.

• The fact is that any kind of abuse we suffered when we were children was not our fault.

• Any kind of abuse where there is a difference of power (worker and boss, patient and doctor, client and therapist, minister and parishoner) is not our fault.

• It doesn't matter if we enjoyed it – the guilt we feel for that is misplaced guilt. If we were sexually aroused, all that shows is that our body did what bodies do – they reacted normally.

• It doesn't matter how many abusers there were: just because most of our family abused us does not prove that it therefore must have been our fault.

Ladybug Bear

As a child I would look for ladybirds in the garden to make them fly home. A children's rhyme says:

Ladybird, Ladybird, fly away home,
Your house is on fire and your children are all burned.

I felt it was so hard on Ladybird. It probably wasn't her fault that her house was on fire, but all her children were dead and gone. The best I could do was send her on her way to see if she could rescue at least one of her little ones.

Ladybug Bear came to me one Christmas and I love her for the way she loved her children, but all of them were burnt and she feels such desperate sadness.

Ladybug has to learn to forgive herself – and that is tough.

Her ladybug cloak is red – red for anger, because anger is important in the early stages of forgiving. I think it is our anger with ourselves that makes us depressed or binge or self-harm or whatever self-destructive thing we are into.

We most desperately need to learn to forgive ourselves, and when I hug Ladybug Bear I try to do a 'forgiveness audit'. Am I letting myself ruminate on the bad things? Am I still holding on to 'It was my fault'?

Strategies for forgiving ourselves

1. Keep reminding yourself that it is not your fault.
2. Accept that the abuse happened and you cannot change the past.
3. Accept that you will be able to become a 'wounded healer' – because of your pain you are likely to become sensitive, caring and able to help others.
4. Treating our body kindly is a huge part of forgiving and loving ourselves. Out with the junk food!

Healing in the community

Any abuse has an effect on the whole family, even on the whole community, not just the abuser and the victim. Sadly for many abused people, if they tell others about the abuse, they can end up being rejected by the rest of the family. This is a tragedy, and sadness and pain come into that family that could take generations to heal.

It is in these kinds of circumstances that forgiveness can transform that sadness into new life and love, but that can take years.

BUT...

Sometimes as I listen to people sharing their pain – their longing to be allowed back into the family/community/church/club – I see someone who seems to have gone through many loops and turns on the helix of forgiveness. Their family may reject them, tell them never to come to the house again, and they can never see their nieces and nephews, and so on. Survivors weep as they talk of their hurt – and then might go on to say, 'I know I should forgive them, but it's hard and I feel so guilty that I can't forgive.'

But every time I listen to this kind of talk, I'm quite sure that the survivor is 'letting go', and is well on the way to forgiving.

Are we 'bitter and twisted'?

As I look around my large circle of friends who are survivors, I don't see 'bitter and twisted' people – even those who insist they cannot or will not forgive.

But they have clearly 'let go'.

True, some of them are a bit 'stuck' and have become over-dependent on others, and seem not to be making much progress (though I can't really know that).

Yes, there is anger.

Yes, there is confusion about forgiving and how it relates to the justice few of us are likely to get.

But I see love and compassion.

I've felt supported and loved, and I know many of my survivor friends are befriending and helping other survivors in court cases and with practical things like finding a safe place to live away from abusers. *All of that I see as forgiveness* – having an attitude of love and care for those around us.

I find it very sad that in survivor groups of Christians, there seem to be more tears shed in discussions about forgiveness than anything else. The very thing that the 'forgive now' people insist will heal us is the very thing that causes the most tears and anguish!

KEY POINTS

■ Forgiving is hard and most survivors seem to struggle with it.

■ Some see forgiving as loss of face or condoning the act.

■ Forgiving ourselves can be tough.

■ Letting go helps us to break our chains and get rid of the negative effects our abuser/s used to have on our life.

CHAIN BREAKING

1. Work at forgiving yourself. Go back to the strategies on page 206 and make a commitment to work at them over the next few weeks.

2. How will you check if you've forgiven yourself? Do you still criticize yourself/apologize too much? Do you still feel it was your fault?

Forgiving ourselves is one of the strongest chains we must break. You might want to get support, perhaps from a self-help group.

Remember
Dump the self-blame!

God knows. God is weeping.

It isn't enough to let bygones be bygones.
ARCHBISHOP DESMOND TUTU

25 Reflections

In this last chapter I'm pulling together the various themes in this book and outlining some reflections for the way ahead.

I went to Australia last year for a healing week at Mayumarri, a centre for abused people, and it was an extraordinary week with a group of delightful people, led by Liz Mullinar. I will weave some of what I learned at Mayumarri into these reflections.

I'd anticipated that in Australia I'd have time to reflect on my chain breaking and pull together the threads in this book. What I hadn't anticipated was the amount of deep emotion I felt, and the consequent healing I experienced.

Rules for life

Although all of us are likely to break our chains in our own unique ways, there seem to be some common elements, for example the power of writing and the huge influence on our life of Inner Child work. (I realized at Mayumarri how I had been neglecting the hurt child within me.)

Communicate with your inner child often – even if it is only ten minutes a day.
LIZ MULLINAR

Of course there are far more 'rules for life' than I can list here, so I hope you might use my list to create your own. Here are my headings:

1. CONNECTING WITH OUR TRUE SELF
Becoming more aware of our inner life helps us to break chains, and we might well find several little children within us. That's OK. I connect with these parts of myself through my creatures.

2. LEARNING TO RELAX, MEDITATE AND TAKE TIME OUT
Think of something specific and lovely, for example, a view, a flower, a psalm, or holding your first cup of tea of the day in your hands and thinking of the hands of God that hold you in love and warmth.

Remember to dance and laugh and pick daisies.

3. RECORDING OUR PROGRESS

Journalling, word wall activities, drawing and painting can all help us to remember our progress, to focus on one change at a time, and to challenge that negative thinking.

4. LIVING WITH OUR INTUITION

Much of our healing is not about logic – it's not necessarily something we can sort out by sitting thinking. We need to let our right brain intuitive side run free to create, and to connect with our soul, our pre-verbal body memories and our Shadow.

5. LEARNING COPING STRATEGIES

Breaking some of our toughest chains could take ages, so coping strategies enable us to get on with our life for now. They have short-term benefits, but in the longer term, we need to go further than just cope. We want to break our chains.

For example, at Mayumarri I learned a most important lesson about the triggers that set me off into freaking out.

Something triggers me (usually through my senses, often smell, or one of the things that freaks me out, such as someone jiggling their leg up and down) and I get overwhelming feelings (anger, sadness etc.). I go into panic mode with adrenalin rushing round my body. I want to escape, but usually I freeze. At this point my usual strategy was to work out what triggered me, but most of the time I was also just blocking those overwhelming feelings – even if I was using positive thinking such as 'It's not Ernie, he's dead, you're safe'.

What Liz taught me is that if I can identify my triggers and my feelings and say those feelings out loud (to someone if I can, or to myself in a mirror), *but also* connect that with my Inner Child (leg jiggling for me means a man getting turned on, which leads in my images to the penis moving in and out of my mouth), then that can release my feelings.

This actual incident happened and as Liz sat with me I felt the release of the feelings. Then Liz said I must empower my Inner Child in some way (little Suzie thought vengeful things about the penis!), or do something creative (I did lots of paintings), or do something physically (we went and smashed plates).

What I had been doing was getting triggered; then the overwhelming feelings were not being dealt with, so they changed within me into fears, phobias, panic attacks, nightmares, negative behaviour such as bingeing and the sense that my life was out of control.

You can follow this in the diagram – and see the differences in the outcomes of the two tracks!

• Follow the blocking track and you get stuck in the nightmares with triggers repeatedly and mysteriously ruining your inner life.

• But if you identify the trigger, talk it out, release the feelings and are empowered by some positive action that feels right for your Inner Child, you enter a transforming moment. You are empowered – and major chain breaking can happen.

And all that can happen because we learned *to listen to our feelings and keep in touch with our Inner Child*.

What Liz, psychotherapist Sue Gerhardt, and neuroscientists such as Louis Cozolino seem to be saying is that we can unlock those trapped memories, so in theory we might one day break all our chains and manage life without need of coping strategies.

Wow! That's a thought that can give us all hope.

6. LEARNING TO TAKE RISKS

The twenty-first century seems to be becoming a risk-free zone, where someone must be blamed for every unfortunate incident, and health and safety rules and regulations get more and more complicated.

We have to learn to take risks if we are to live a fulfilling life – risk the new relationship, risk going for the much better job.

I took a risk by writing this book and the process has been long, painful and very confusing. I couldn't have done it without my survivor friends around me taking risks, sharing their feelings and their stories. Take a risk and go for it. Yes, accidents and bad things might happen – but they do anyway in life. Throw off your chains and get out there!

7. ACKNOWLEDGING OUR ANGER

Given time to reflect on my childhood while I was at Mayumarri, I found some unexpected anger welling up in me. My blank feelings about my step-father metamorphosed into rage as the week went on and as I sensed that I was 'held' and loved by the carers.

I knew about this blankness and didn't know whether it meant that

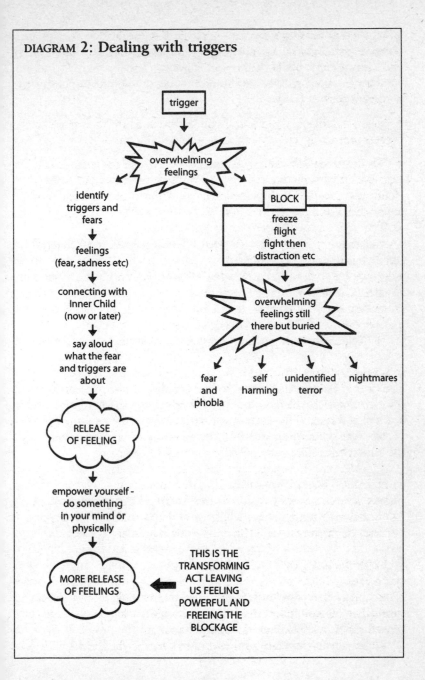

DIAGRAM 2: Dealing with triggers

trigger

overwhelming feelings

identify triggers and fears

feelings (fear, sadness etc)

connecting with Inner Child (now or later)

say aloud what the fear and triggers are about

RELEASE OF FEELING

empower yourself - do something in your mind or physically

MORE RELEASE OF FEELINGS

BLOCK

freeze
flight
fight then
distraction etc

overwhelming feelings still there but buried

fear and phobia

self harming

unidentified terror

nightmares

THIS IS THE TRANSFORMING ACT LEAVING US FEELING POWERFUL AND FREEING THE BLOCKAGE

I was beyond the anger and letting go, or if it meant that the rage was trapped within me. Discovering a punch bag was my way through my constrained rage – and by the last day there I found myself running, screaming, laughing, free to shout and punch at the injustice of the way I was treated as a child.

The post-punching calmness felt good. I felt at peace – and that peace has stayed with me.

8. BECOMING THE PERSON WE WANT TO BE
I've wondered over the years whether we can become the person we were *meant* to be – the person we would have become without the abuse. But I'm not sure we can become that person.

We can become the person we *want* to be.

I used to wonder with Ruth what I would have been like if she had been my mother – no doubt I'd be quite different. But we need to be wary of wandering too far into 'what if' and 'if only'. These are two little phrases that can seriously ruin our life.

9. LEARNING TO BE CONTENT
Appreciating what we have is healing. Constantly harping on about what we haven't got is damaging.

Loud, envious and angry survivors can give the impression that their abuse is the worst thing in the world. That isn't necessarily so. Think of war-torn Africa and the Middle East. Of course wars are abusive, but what I'm getting at is that we need to dump our 'the world owes me a living' attitude and develop a sense of contentment in our situation.

10. FORGIVING IS HEALING
Most of us won't get justice. Most of us won't get an apology. So the best thing to do to improve the quality of our life is to 'let go'.

Over the four years of writing this book I found that 'time has been a good healer'. I know I forgave my mother and older brother long ago, and now I know I've 'let go' of my resentments about my uncle and step-father.

I think that by attending to the small moments in my life of being a loving, forgiving and caring person, the bigger events have lost their power. My step-father and uncle no longer have the power to keep me trapped in chains of anger and recrimination.

OK, I got no justice – but I'm heading for a happier life.

I believe that this 'letting go' is helping me to heal as I go on working at rejecting my ruminations of resentments, changing them into the more positive images of beauty (the amazing rainbow that signals the end of the storm) and of the future (the people in our self-help group whom we can reach out to). This is how we find joy and peace.

Life might not have been all that great so far, but we can get out there and make our life extraordinary and purposeful.

11. LEARNING THROUGHOUT OUR LIVES

Abuse can teach us so much. Even an awful triggering moment can be seen as a way of unlocking the past.

I'm not saying the abuse was good, but I am saying that we can take our past and transform it into something beautiful. We can become a 'wounded healer' – not dragging survivors screaming towards healing, but with our hand stretched out to help, perhaps by sending a quick text message or email.

12. ACCEPTING THAT WE WILL HAVE SET BACKS

We're bound to have slip-ups – they are part of being human, they are learning experiences. Analyse what went wrong and work out how not to make the same mistake again.

If you are like me and you have major 'crashes' such as weeping for hours, or sometimes being unable to face something you said you'd do, that unpredictability can be a part of our 'shadow', and we may be unable to work out at times what is going on. I know I can be unreliable. I know I can't always predict when I'm going to 'crash'.

But as I break chains, so I'm getting a sense of being able to control my life more and accept and deal positively with my set backs.

13. ACCEPTING THAT WE'VE COME FROM A TERRIBLE PLACE

At Mayumarri Liz asked the group which of us had contemplated or tried suicide. Everyone's hand went up – carers as well. It was an astonishing moment. I felt such love for that group of people. We'd all shared a similar path.

We aren't feeble, or stupid, or hopeless because we contemplate suicide. We're normal human beings who have been violated.

But we heal.

14. LIVING CREATIVELY

Getting our right brain active by being creative is one of the most healing things we can do. In our S:VOX self-help groups for survivors of abuse we play with glitter and glue, we dress up, we explore beauty and fun in order to heal our damaged inner world.

We touch our small hurting child as we blow bubbles and some of us learn that we can play and still be safe. We can laugh and not be physically beaten. We can giggle and even make mistakes but still be loved and valued.

15. NOT DEMONIZING OUR ABUSERS

Almost inevitably our abusers were hurting people whose lives were screwed up by someone in their past. Of course what they did was wrong, and some of them are probably evil and dangerous, but if we make them out to be demonic monsters we might be warping our own thinking. There is little point in hating them, or hanging on to images in our mind of what they did (but of course we hate them in the early stages of uncovering our past).

We might find we can't completely forgive them, but setting out to let it all go might lead to a surprise in the long term.

Some of the pain may never go. But there is no place in our life for long term-hatred and bitterness.

16. LEARNING NOT TO GET STUCK

Because it can be difficult to recover from trauma, there is always the danger that we might get stuck, and end up sitting in the midst of our chains feeling helpless.

We can become over-dependent on others (although of course leaning on someone for a while so they can help you break your chains is good). Leaning too heavily on people can stop us learning to be appropriately independent and gritting our teeth as we determinedly head for healing.

The trouble is I sometimes smile to myself and wonder if there is something to be gained by staying hurt and fragile. When I can't cope with something, David helps me. What would be the implications for my life if I heal more? (I might be left with no excuse to binge on chocolate and I might have to accept that I am strong enough to go out into the crowd! Oh dear – it's rather comfortable where I am thank you!)

17. ACCEPTING YOU MAY NEVER KNOW

I accept that I may never know exactly what happened. That's OK. I've learned that there are many of us who have memories so vague that they are no more than a 'feeling' – an intuitive sense that all was not well back then.

That doesn't make those intuitive feelings wrong. Some people shout very loudly that most memories of abuse are made up. This just isn't true. Of course some might be. But apparently that kind of fiction is rare.

If, like mine, your memories are intangible and vague, focus on learning to cope with your difficulties (such as anxiety) and do some serious chain breaking – working with your Inner Child and so on. Get a teddy.

You may never know the whole truth. What's important is not to get trapped in a low quality of life. 'Let go' – and learn to dance or take up snowboarding or set your mind on finding peace and joy in your world.

18. KNOWING WE'RE ABLE JUST TO BEAR IT

And that is 'goodenough'.

19. LEARNING WHAT MATTERS MOST IN LIFE

Some people who recover from cancer talk of how the illness and their possible imminent death helped them to see how valuable friends and family are, and how important it is to spend time with those we love.

It isn't money, status, power and so on that give our lives meaning – it is much more the moment our new baby is put into our arms, the day a frightened survivor first speaks at the self-help group, the experience of watching a lily come into bloom and the soft surge of emotion we feel when we read a poem.

20. WORKING OUT WHAT KIND OF PERSON WE WANT TO BE

Do we want to be the angry, resentful person who gives out negative messages that repel people? Or do we want to be known as Maud was?

I know the way she went
Home with her maiden posy,
For her feet have touch'd the meadows
And left the daisies rosy.
ALFRED LORD TENNYSON

21. TAKING ONE DAY AT A TIME

One day (or ten minutes) at a time. That's all we can do. We make our life too stressful if today we worry too much about tomorrow, or next week.

The way to move on is always the next step – however long the journey. That's how we break chains – one chain at a time – one day at a time – ten minutes at a time.

22. PULLING TOGETHER

Just as the Emperor penguins survive by group cooperation, so survivors can pull together. Bullies are defeated when a group stands up to them. As time goes on and abuse is talked about more, so abusers will have fewer places to hide and their power to keep secrets and demand silence from their victims will be diminished.

We can make a better future for our children if we learn to stick together – we make our communities safer places.

Weak things united become strong.
THOMAS FULLER

23. FOCUSING ON EMPOWERMENT

My 'don't break the law' strategy – which I've found so successful in the last few weeks to stop my chaotic eating (see chapter 12) – is actually about empowerment. I was talking through my sudden unexpected ability to control my eating with Kate last week and I identified the reason why this strategy was working. Previously I was saying to myself, 'There are brownies in the cake tin and I will eat several of them because I am too weak willed not to.' In other words I was believing the 'I'm hopeless' stuff.

By changing that negative thinking I was empowering myself. 'I don't steal from the supermarket – I don't binge on chocolate. I can have some sometimes, it's not forbidden, but the bingeing is forbidden and I have the power to control myself.' (I hope I'm not being too negative in acknowledging as I write this that it might not last! No way am I giving up chocolate – what a hideous thought. But I'm trying hard not to binge.)

Identifying and challenging our negative thinking is so very important, but as I reflect on that, I wonder how much of my out-of-character ability to control my eating at the moment is because I'm now much more aware of my Inner Child? I'm aware I've broken chains. I know I'm healing. I can look back on the last few months after being at Mayumarri and know that I can stand in the queue to buy a train ticket, as I did this morning, and not worry that there are people behind me.

Focus on empowerment – it works.

24. OPENING YOUR SOUL TO THE MUSIC OF THE STARS

There is so much more to life than birth, worry, death, then rotting in our grave. If we open our souls we experience love, wonder, contentment, and the joy of 'story'. All life is about 'story', so tell yours. Listen to others.

Taking opportunities to read novels, watch films, let our soul soar with music – all this helps us to glimpse something beyond the physical world.

> *What [movies do] is give you an experience of transcendence. They let you lose yourself in somebody else's story. And sometimes in losing yourself you find yourself, or at least a part of yourself. It may be a part of yourself that you didn't even know needed finding. It may be… a part that needed to go back and become a child again. A part that needed to understand, maybe, or forgive.*
> KEN GIRE

25. MAKING A PLAN FOR A BETTER LIFE

As you end this book, consider how you might:

• avoid self-sabotaging any good or positive work you will have done by working through it (for example, when you next 'crash', deciding that you are hopeless and are never going to heal)
• record in some way your positive feelings at breaking some chains
• decide to choose one part of the book each week for the next couple of months and work more on those aspects of your healing
• share your progress with someone.

26. LIVING WITH A HIGHER POWER

Many recovery programmes are based on our acknowledgment that there is a Higher Power in this universe, and learning that there is power out there to change our lives for the better can be a central part of our recovery.

Love is the most universal understanding of spiritual power; it underpins all that is done at Mayumarri. I would go as far as to say that *love is the reason for living*. Many religions point to a God of love, and if you merge those two ideas you end up with:

God who is love is the reason for living

and also…

God who is love gives me a reason for living

and also…

When I know God I know love

and you can turn that into…

God loves me.

CHAIN BREAKING

1. List those healing strategies that you think helped you most:

- Journalling
- Painting/drawing/modelling
- Inner Child non-dominant hand writing/drawing
- Making a scrap book or some kind of good memory box or shelf
- Meditating on being 'held' in the loving arms of God
- Reminding yourself you're goodenough.

You could make a plan for breaking the rest of your chains using these most helpful strategies.

2. Which of the 'rules for life' listed in this chapter most appeal to you? Which ones annoy you? Do you know why they annoy you?

3. Look back at the diagram about responding to triggers on page 211. Can you make a commitment to breaking the chains you are held in by your overpowering emotions?

4. Write or draw about you – the good, unique, loved and valuable person. Do you need to work more on raising your self-esteem?

5. Remember those big decisions, sitting on the end of your bed – 'Do I want to be like this for the rest of my life?'

No!

How can you make today 'the first day of the rest of your life'?

Further Resources

Dealing with a crisis
If you are in crisis and live in the UK you can ring the Samaritans at any time. Their number is 0845 7909090.

Childline in the UK offers help to any child needing to talk: 0800 1111.

NSPCC in the UK offers help to anyone concerned that a child is at risk: 0808 8005000.

Self-help groups and other sources of healing
If you live in the UK a new organization S:VOX (survivors' voices) runs self-help weekends, and aims to start nationwide self-help groups for survivors and those who support them. Write to them c/o St James' Church, 236 Mitcham Lane, London, SW16 6NT or click on their website to join and to see if there is already a group in your area.
    www.svox.org.uk

If you live in Australia, click onto
    www.mayumarri.com.au or http://asca.org.au

DABS (Directory and Book Services) sell a National Directory listing over 800 organizations in the UK and Ireland related to childhood abuse and sexual abuse. Their address is: 17, Upper Belgrave Road, Clifton, Bristol, BS8 2XH. Tel: 0117 923 9318.
    www.dabsbooks.co.uk

The Samaritans give useful advice on a range of issues such as mental distress and dealing with self-harm.
    www.samaritans.org.uk

MIND is a mental health charity that supports those in mental distress. You may find your local MIND group can support you.
    www.mind.org.uk

Depression Alliance offers support for those who are depressed and those who support them.
www.depressionalliance.org.uk

Help with self-harming
www.lifesigns.org.uk/
www.siari.co.uk
www.selfharm.org.uk/

Help with dissociating
First Person Plural, PO Box 2537, Wolverhampton, WV4 4ZL.
www.firstpersonplural.org.uk
www.ukssd.org (for a wide range of services offered on many problems survivors have).

Help with eating disorders
Eating Disorders Association (EDA). Tel: 0845 634 1414.
www.edauk.com

Help for both survivors and supporters
For a really useful source of information leaflets and support for a whole range of difficulties survivors have, contact: Bristol Crisis Service for Women, PO Box 654, Bristol, BS99 1XH
www.users.zetnet.co.uk

A study and support group for those working in the areas of trauma, abuse and dissociative disorders:
TAG, PO Box 465, Godalming, Surrey, GU72 2YL

Jane Chevous' book (see over) has an extensive resources section listing helpful agencies useful for survivors and carers, as well as sources of research on abuse.

Puppets and dolls
If you can't find just the doll you want in general toy shops, you might want to search for a special doll on the web. I found mine in Hamleys. (The more lifelike dolls do tend to be expensive.)

Large puppets can be much cheaper than a lifelike doll and these are easy to find on the web at www.puppetsbypost.com.

Kumquat puppets are particularly good – so delightful they are easy to bond with.

Help for men

www.malesurvivor.org

www.svox.org.uk

The following books may also be helpful:

Mike Lew, *Victims no longer: men recovering from incest and other sexual and child abuse*, Harper Collins

Mike Lew, *Leaping upon the mountains*, Small Wonder Books. (This book has a useful international resources section for men.)

Books for further reading

Dr Roger Baker, *Understanding panic attacks and overcoming fear*, Lion Hudson

Lucia Capacchione, *Recover of Your Inner Child*, Simon and Schuster

Jane Chevous, *From Silence to Sanctuary*, SPCK

Louis Cozolino, *The neuroscience of psychotherapy*, WW Norton and Co

Susan Forward, *Emotional Blackmail*, Harper Collins

Sue Gerhardt, *Why Love Matters: how affection shapes a baby's brain*, Routledge

Judith Herman, *Trauma and recovery*, Basic Books

Jo Ind, *Fat is a Spiritual Issue*, Mowbray

Susan Jeffers, *End the Struggle and Dance with Life*, Hodder and Stoughton

D., S., and M Linn, *Don't forgive too soon*, Paulist Press

Kate Litchfield, *Tend my flock*, Canterbury Press

John Monbourquette, *How to befriend your shadow*, Darton, Longman and Todd

Russ Parker, *Healing Dreams*, SPCK

Babette Rothschild, *The Body Remembers*, W. W. Norton and Company

Dorothy Rowe, *Depression: the way out of your prison*, Routledge and Kegan Paul

Dorothy Rowe, *Friends and Enemies*, Harper Collins

Carroll Saussy, *The Gift of Anger,* Louisville: Westminster John Knox

Steve Shaw, *Dancing with your Shadow,* Triangle

Marilee Strong, *A Bright Red Scream,* Penguin Books

Charles Whitfield, *Boundaries and Relationships,* Health Communications, Inc

Philip Yancey, *What's So Amazing About Grace?,* Zondervan

Workbooks

Laura Davis, *The courage to heal work book,* Harper and Row

Robert Kelly and Fay Maxted, *The Survivor's Guide,* Rugby RoSa (www.survivorguide.co.uk)

Autobiography

Alice Sebold, *Lucky,* Picador

Jill Saward, *Rape: my Story,* Pan Books

Transactional Analysis

Eric Berne, *Games people play,* Penguin

Thomas A. Harris, *I'm OK, you're OK,* Pan Books

Finding a counsellor

Ideally ask around your local area and self-help group.

Alternatively contact: The British Association for Counselling and Psychotherapy, BACP House, 53-7 Albert Street, Rugby, CV21 2SG.

Tel: 0870 443 5252.
www.bacp.co.uk

Or go onto the ukssd site:
www.ukssd.org

All Lion books are available from your local
bookshop, or can be ordered via our website
or from Marston Book Services. For a free
catalogue, showing the complete list of titles
available, please contact:

Customer Services
Marston Book Services
PO Box 269
Abingdon
Oxon
OX14 4YN

Tel: 01235 465500
Fax: 01235 465555

Our website can be found at:
www.lionhudson.com